HAL LEONARD BASS METHOD

BASS ARPEGGIO FINDER

Easy-to-Use Guide to Over 1,300 Bass Arpeggios

BY CHAD JOHNSON

ISBN 0-634-07329-X

In Australia Contact:
Hal Leonard Australia Pty. Ltd
22 Taunton Drive P.O. Box 5130
Cheltenham East, 3192 Victoria, Australia
Email: ausadmin@halleonard.com

Visit Hal Leonard Online at www.halleonard.com

HAL•LEONARD® CORPORATION
7777 W. BLUEMOUND RD. P.O. BOX 13819 MILWAUKEE, WI 53213

TABLE OF CONTENTS

INTRODUCTION

Bass Arpeggio Finder is an extensive reference guide to over 1,300 arpeggio shapes. Twenty-eight different qualities are covered for each key, and each quality is presented in four different shapes. Open strings are used when possible, but most of the shapes are moveable, and therefore easily transposed to any key. The shapes are shown first with a sixth-string root, then with a fifth-string root. Since shapes built off the fifth string are essentially the same shape as those built off the sixth string, the fifth-string shapes have been extended to include notes on the sixth string when practical. When playing through the fifth-string shapes, however, you should still begin on the fifth string, as this is the root of the arpeggio. The notes on the sixth string should be included as an extension of the shape.

A fingerboard chart of the bass neck is provided below for reference. If you're unfamiliar with the notes on the neck, you can use this chart when transposing the shapes to new keys.

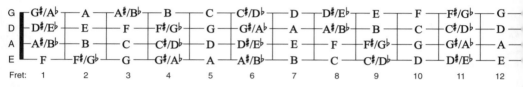

G	G♯/A♭	A	A♯/B♭	B	C	C♯/D♭	D	D♯/E♭	E	F	F♯/G♭	G
D	D♯/E♭	E	F	F♯/G♭	G	G♯/A♭	A	A♯/B♭	B	C	C♯/D♭	D
A	A♯/B♭	B	C	C♯/D♭	D	D♯/E♭	E	F	F♯/G♭	G	G♯/A♭	A
E	F	F♯/G♭	G	G♯/A♭	A	A♯/B♭	B	C	C♯/D♭	D	D♯/E♭	E
Fret: 1	2	3	4	5	6	7	8	9	10	11	12

The arpeggios throughout this book are presented in a grid fashion. In case you're not familiar with this type of notation, below is a detailed explanation of how they're read. The four vertical lines represent the four strings of the bass. They are arranged low to high from left to right.

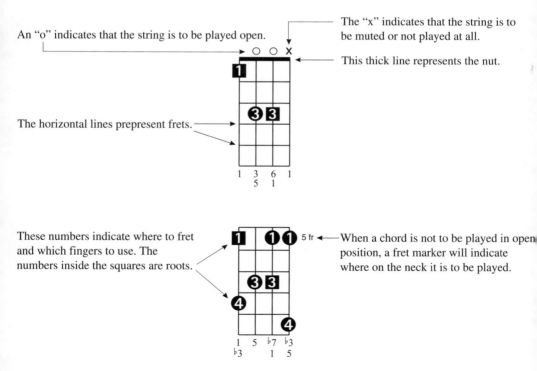

The "x" indicates that the string is to be muted or not played at all.

An "o" indicates that the string is to be played open.

This thick line represents the nut.

The horizontal lines prepresent frets.

These numbers indicate where to fret and which fingers to use. The numbers inside the squares are roots.

When a chord is not to be played in open position, a fret marker will indicate where on the neck it is to be played.

BUILDING ARPEGGIOS

This section is intended to provide a basic knowledge of arpeggios, how to build them, and how to play them. Some of you may already know this; if so, skip ahead! If not, read on and learn how to impress your friends who don't know.

WHAT IS AN ARPEGGIO?

An arpeggio can be defined simply as the notes of a chord played separately—as a melody. In other words, instead of sounding the chord by plucking or strumming all of the strings at once, the notes are played one at a time. This can be done from highest to lowest, lowest to highest, or in any order you choose. Since arpeggios are constructed from chord tones (because they basically are chords), we'll first need to know how to build chords before tackling the shapes.

TRIADS

A chord is simply a collection of notes deliberately arranged in a harmonious (or sometimes non-harmonious) fashion. The most common type of chord is called a triad. The name triad is telling of the number of notes in the chord—three. Triads are usually found as one of four different qualities: major, minor, augmented, or diminished. Below, we find what's known as a C Major triad:

The words "root," "third," and "fifth" below the notes on the staff indicate how each note is functioning within

the chord. A root note is the foundation of the chord and the note after which the chord will be named.

INTERVALS

The other two notes in our C triad (the 3rd and the 5th) are responsible for the *quality* of the chord. The notes C and E are an interval (or distance) of a major 3rd apart. Intervals are comprised of two components: a *number* and a *quality*.

In the case of the number, we can determine that C to E is a *3rd* by simply counting through the musical alphabet. Starting from C: C is one, D is two, and E is three. (The word "root" is many times used interchangeably with the number "1." For all practical purposes, they mean the same thing.) From C to G is a 5th, and we can confirm this by again counting up from C: C(1)–D(2)–E(3)–F(4)–G(5).

Determining the quality of an interval is not quite as easy as the number, but it's not too difficult. It will require a bit of memorization, but it's very logical. Below we'll find all twelve of the notes in the chromatic scale and their intervals measured from a C root note:

This example tells us a great deal about intervals. We can see a few formulas here at work. The first thing we should notice is that a minor interval is always one half step smaller than a major interval. C to E is a major 3rd, whereas C to E♭ is a minor 3rd. C to A is a major 6th, whereas C to A♭ is a minor 6th, etc. The next thing we should notice is how 4ths and 5ths work. We can see that an augmented interval is always one half step greater than a perfect one, and a diminished interval is always one half step smaller.

Any triad of one of the four above-mentioned qualities will contain a root, 3rd, and 5th. Other types of triads you may encounter include 6 chords, sus4 chords, and sus2 chords. Theses chords are the product of (in the case of sus4 and sus2 chords) replacing the 3rd with another note or (in the case of 6 chords) replacing the 5th (or sometimes adding to it) with another note.

Below are several different qualities of triads which will allow us to examine these intervals at work and note how they affect the names of these chords:

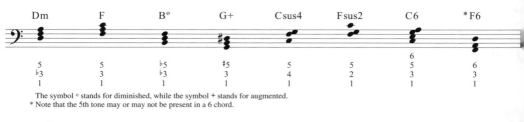

The symbol ° stands for diminished, while the symbol + stands for augmented.
* Note that the 5th tone may or may not be present in a 6 chord.

7TH CHORDS

Beyond the triad, we'll encounter many more chords, most commonly 7th chords. These chords will not only contain the root, 3rd, and 5th, but also the 7th. Below are a few common 7th chords. (Note that the 7th interval can be major or minor independently of the 3rd, thus affecting the name of the chord.)

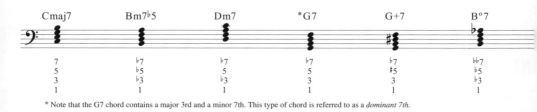

* Note that the G7 chord contains a major 3rd and a minor 7th. This type of chord is referred to as a *dominant 7th*.

EXTENSIONS

Finally, beyond 7th chords, we have extensions. The concept of extensions is a bit complicated and will only be touched upon here, as it requires more extensive study than is possible within the scope of this book. Basically, extended chords continue the process of stacking notes onto a triad that we began with the 7th chord. Instead of only adding the 7th to the chord, however, in a 9th chord we'll add the 7th and the 9th. In an 11th chord, we'll add the 7th, 9th, and 11th to our triad, etc. Now, here's the catch: not all of these notes need to be present in an extended chord. The general rule is, if the 7th is present, then notes other than the root, 3rd, and 5th are extensions and therefore numbered an octave higher (9, 11, 13). The C13 chord on the next page demonstrates this concept:

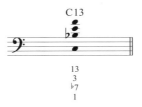

C13

13
3
♭7
1

Note that there is no 5th (G) present in this chord, but the presence of the 7th (B-flat) tells us that this chord is called C13, rather than some kind of C6 chord.

Now that you know how to build chords, you're ready to start adding arpeggios to your arsenal. The following pages contain some of the most common shapes, applicable to just about any playing style.

PLAYING ARPEGGIOS

When playing the notes of a chord one after another in arpeggiated fashion, you may decide to omit some notes for reasons of musical taste. For demonstration purposes the examples in this book have all possible notes included at least once unless otherwise stated.

You'll find there are other possible fingerings you may prefer over our suggested ones. For instance, when consecutive notes on the same fret occur on different strings, you may decide to use a different finger for each to get a smooth, even sound. Or you may execute a finger roll. Rather than picking up the fingertip to move to the next note, allow the finger to relax at the last joint, rolling the pad of the finger down to play the note about 3/8" below the tip. When playing the notes in the opposite order, you'll need to plan ahead by starting out with your finger in this flattened position for the higher note, then raising it so the tip rolls onto the lower note.

Now that you know how to build chords and play them as arpeggios, you're ready to start adding some arpeggios to your arsenal. The following pages contain some of the most common shapes, applicable to just about any playing style.

ARPEGGIO QUALITIES

Below is a list of the twenty-eight different arpeggio qualities presented in this book, their abbreviations, and their formulas:

CHORD TYPE	ABBREVIATION	FORMULA
Major	C	1–3–5
Minor	Cm	1–$\flat$3–5
Augmented	C+	1–3–$\sharp$5
Diminished	C°	1–$\flat$3–$\flat$5
Fifth (Power Chord)	C5	1–5
Added Ninth	Cadd9	1–3–5–9
Minor Added Ninth	Cm(add9)	1–$\flat$3–5–9
Suspended Fourth	Csus4	1–4–5
Suspended Second	Csus2	1–2–5
Sixth	C6	1–3–5–6
Minor Sixth	Cm6	1–$\flat$3–5–6
Major Seventh	Cmaj7	1–3–5–7
Major Ninth	Cmaj9	1–3–5–7–9
Minor Seventh	Cm7	1–$\flat$3–5–$\flat$7
Minor, Major Seventh	Cm(maj7)	1–$\flat$3–5–7
Minor Seventh, Flat Fifth	Cm7$\flat$5	1–$\flat$3–$\flat$5–$\flat$7
Minor Ninth	Cm9	1–$\flat$3–5–$\flat$7–9
Minor Eleventh	Cm11	1–$\flat$3–5–$\flat$7–9–11
Seventh	C7	1–3–5–$\flat$7
Seventh, Suspended Fourth	C7sus4	1–4–5–$\flat$7
Augmented Seventh	C+7	1–3–$\sharp$5–$\flat$7
Seventh, Flat Fifth	C7$\flat$5	1–3–$\flat$5–$\flat$7
Ninth	C9	1–3–5–$\flat$7–9
Seventh, Sharp Ninth	C7$\sharp$9	1–3–5–$\flat$7–$\sharp$9
Seventh, Flat Ninth	C7$\flat$9	1–3–5–$\flat$7–$\flat$9
Eleventh	C11	1–3–5–$\flat$7–9–11*
Thirteenth	C13	1–3–5–$\flat$7–9–11–13**
Diminished Seventh	C°7	1–$\flat$3–$\flat$5–$\flat\flat$7

---

*   The 3rd is sometimes omitted from an eleventh chord.
** The 11th is sometimes omitted from a thirteenth chord.

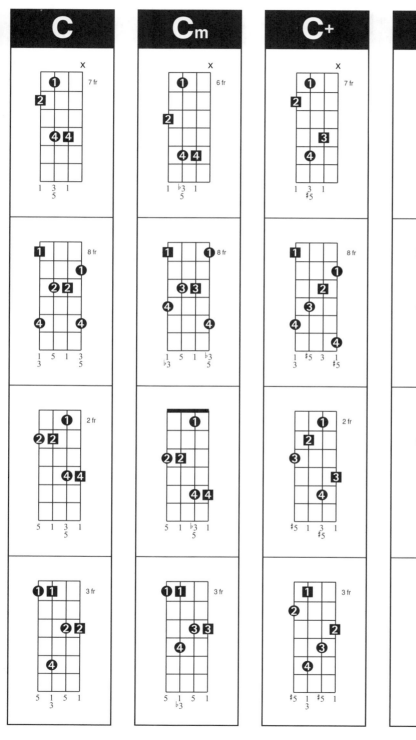

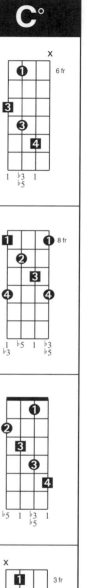

C5   Cadd9   Cm(add9)   Csus4

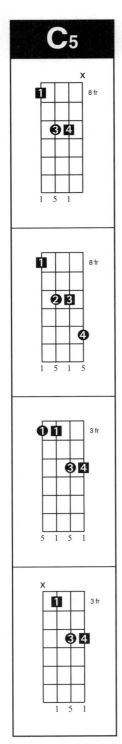

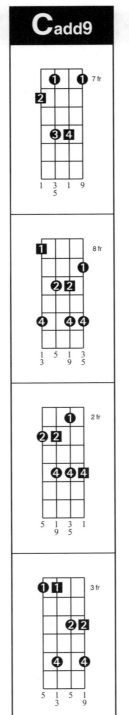

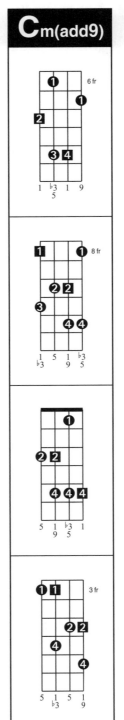

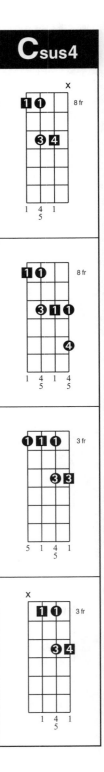

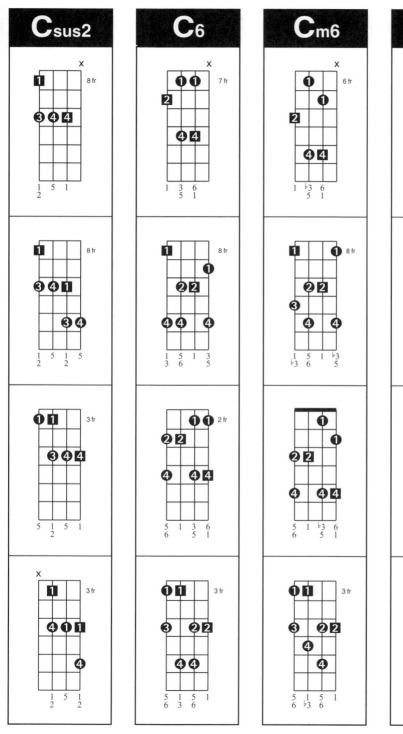

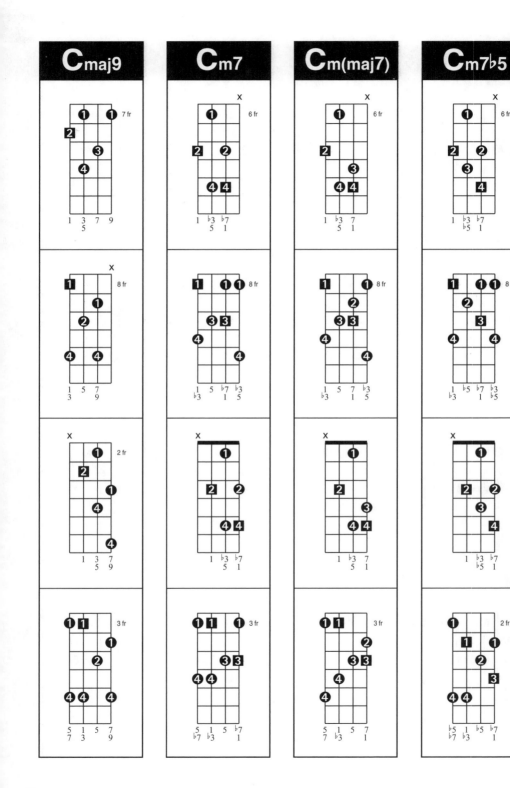

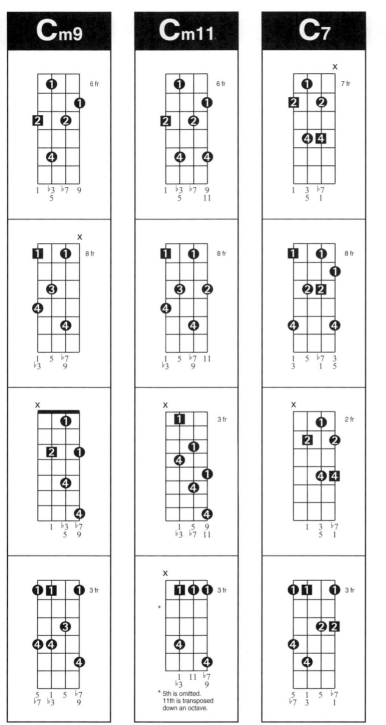

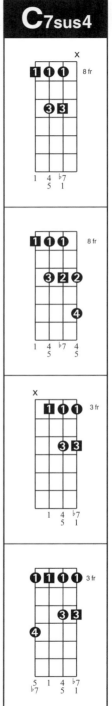

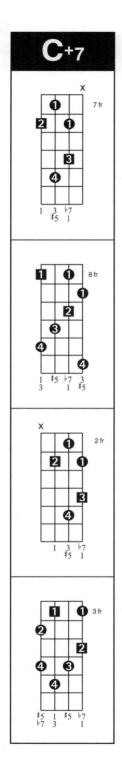
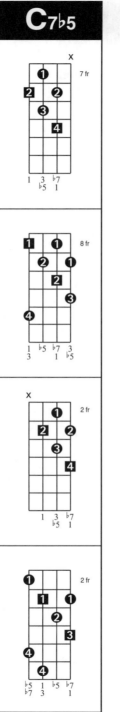
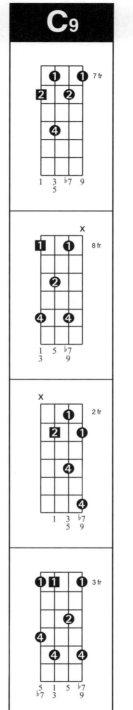
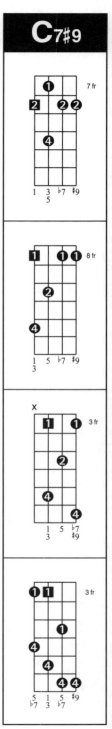

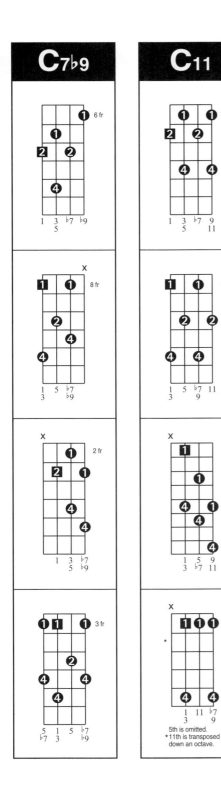

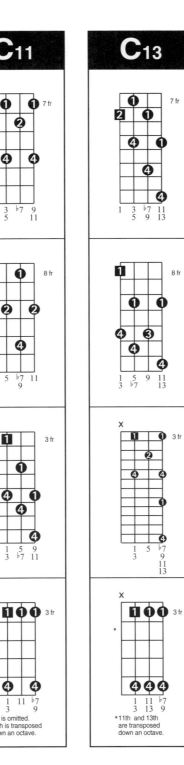

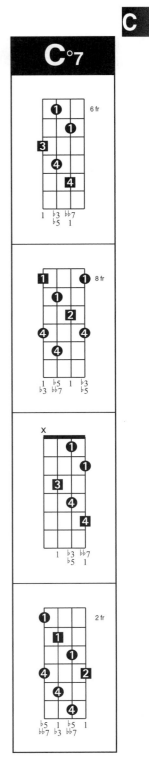

C7♭9

6 fr

1 3 ♭7 ♭9
   5

x

8 fr

1 5 ♭7
3   ♭9

x

2 fr

1 3 ♭7
   5 ♭9

3 fr

5 1 5 ♭7
♭7 3   ♭9

C11

7 fr

1 3 ♭7 9
   5   11

8 fr

1 5 ♭7 11
3   9

x

3 fr

1 5 9
3 ♭7 11

x

3 fr

1 11 ♭7
3   9

5th is omitted.
*11th is transposed
down an octave.

C13

7 fr

1 3 ♭7 11
   5 9   13

8 fr

1 5 9 11
3 ♭7   13

x

3 fr

1 5 ♭7
3
   9
   11
   13

x

3 fr

1 11 ♭7
3 13 9

*11th and 13th
are transposed
down an octave.

C°7

6 fr

1 ♭3 ♭♭7
   ♭5 1

8 fr

1 ♭5 1 ♭3
♭3 ♭♭7   ♭5

x

1 ♭3 ♭♭7
   ♭5 1

2 fr

♭5 1 ♭5 1
♭♭7 ♭3 ♭♭7

15

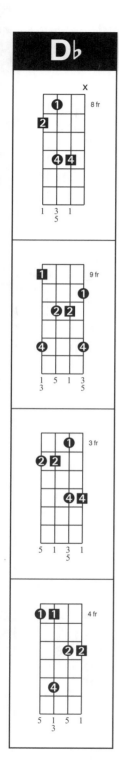
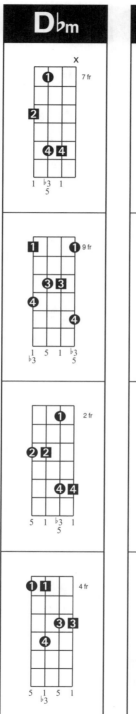
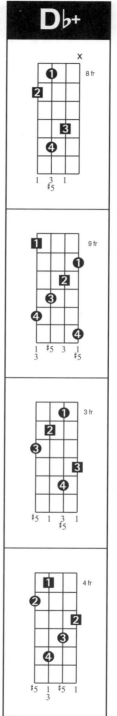
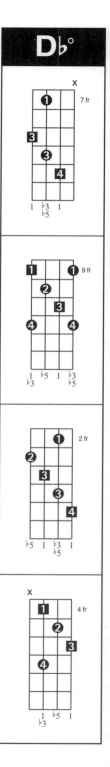

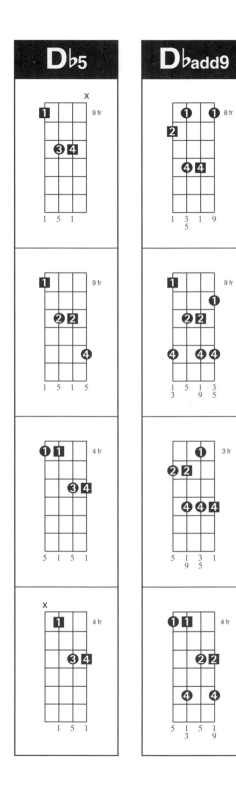

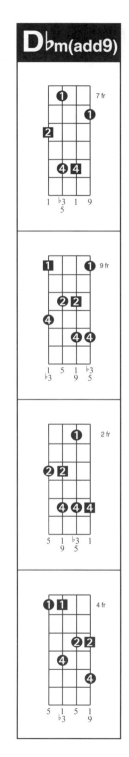

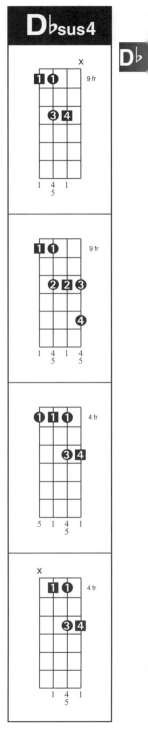

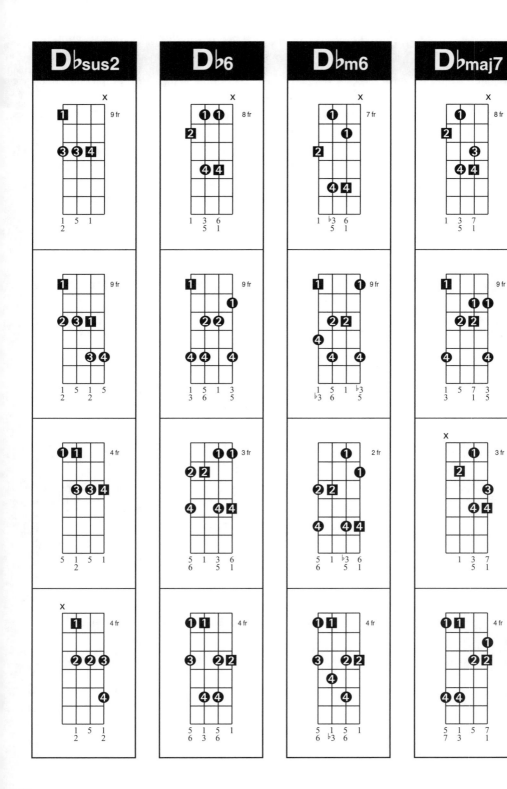

D♭sus2   D♭6   D♭m6   D♭maj7

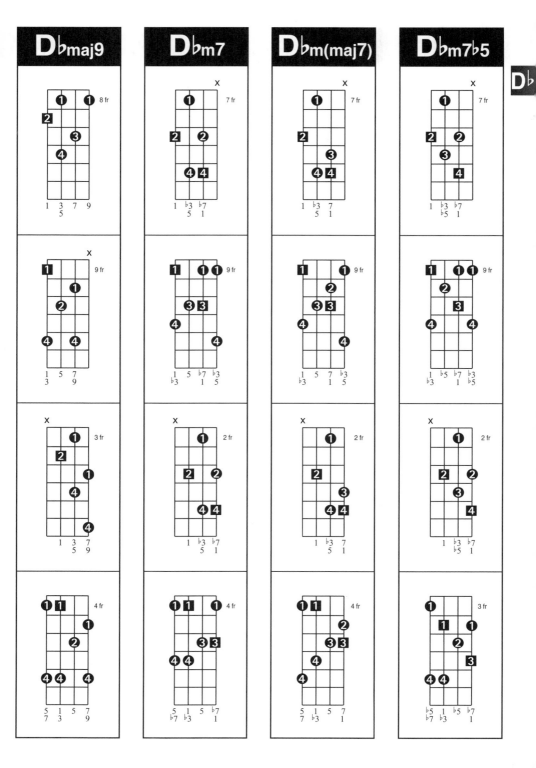

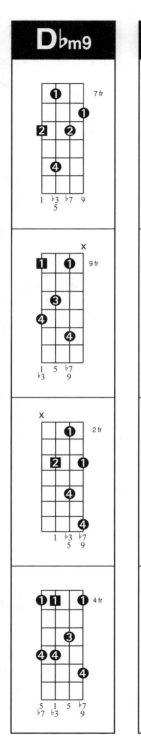

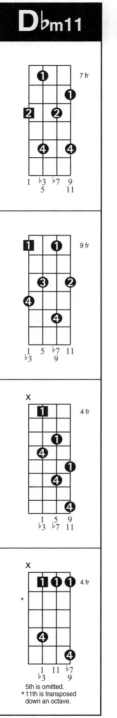

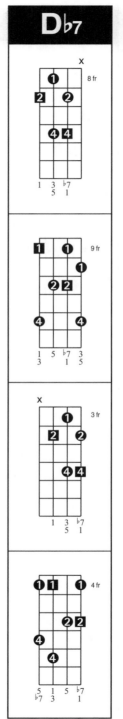

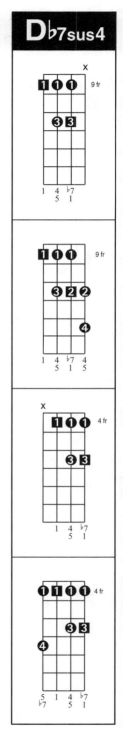

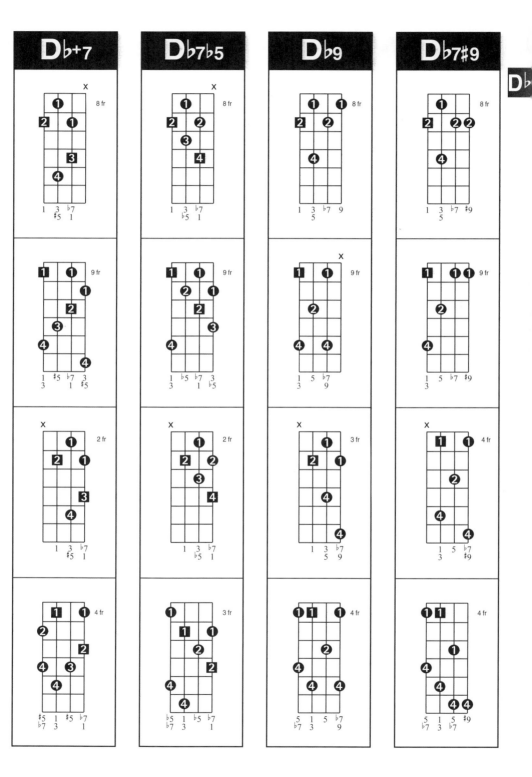

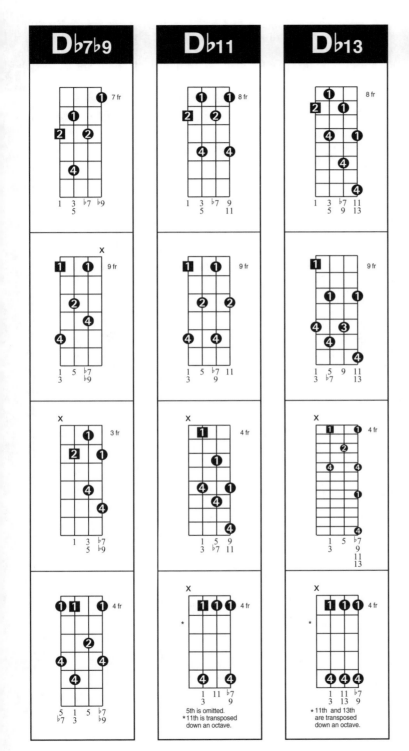
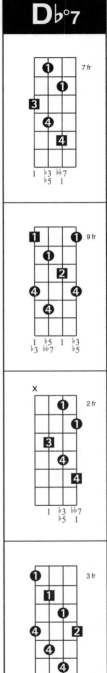

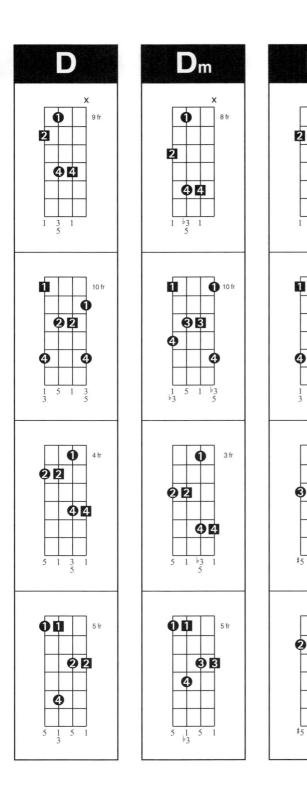

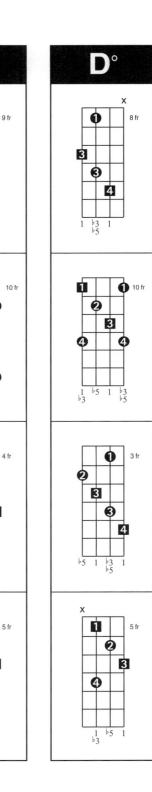

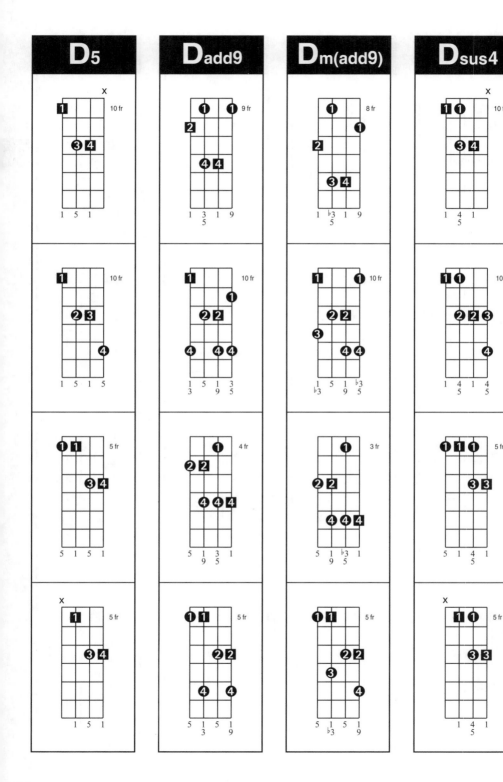

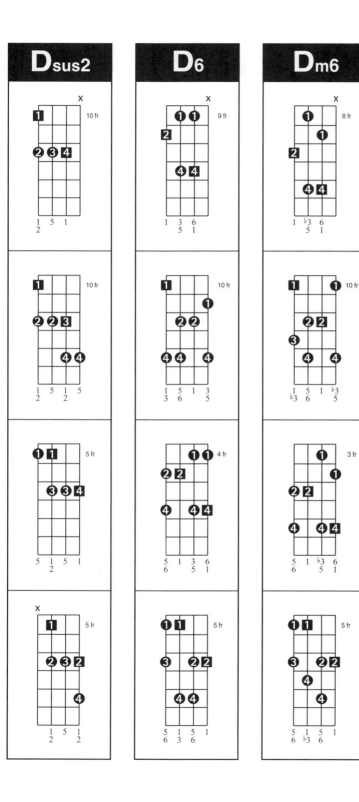

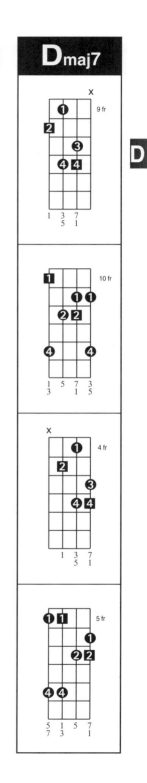

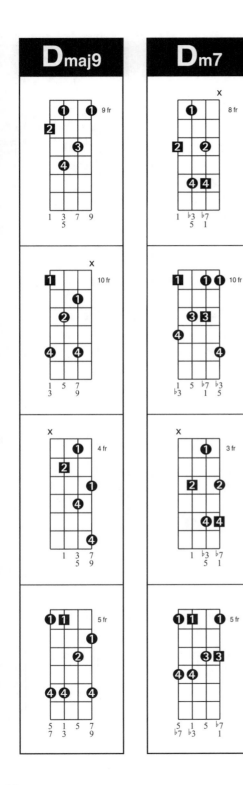
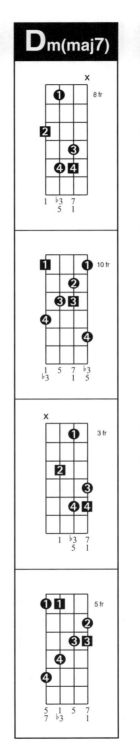
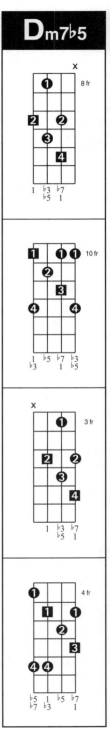

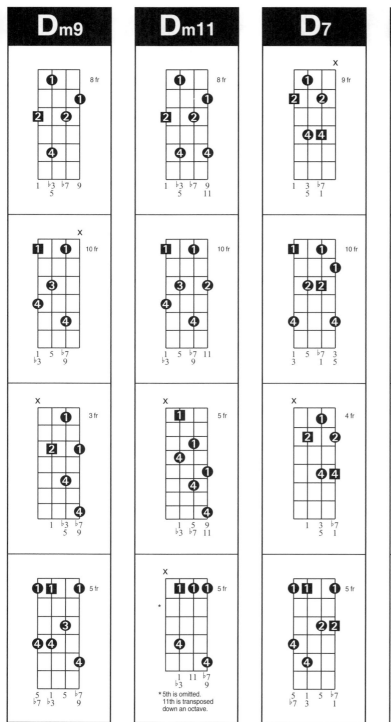

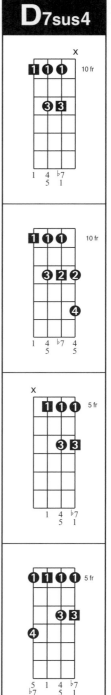

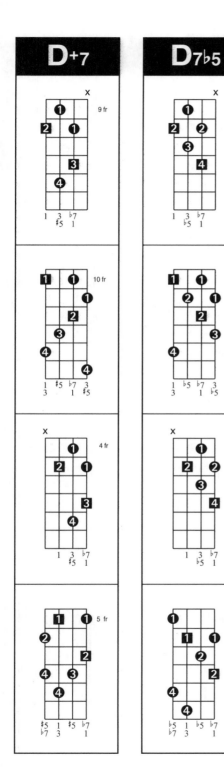
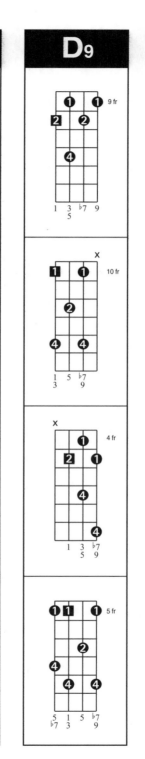
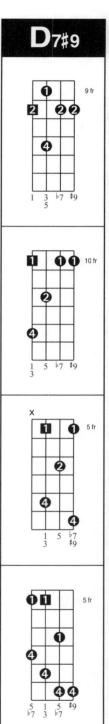

D7♭9

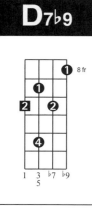

8 fr

1 3 ♭7 ♭9
  5

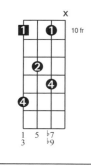

x 10 fr

1 5 ♭7
3 ♭9

x 4 fr

1 3 ♭7
5 ♭9

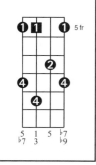

5 fr

5 1 5 ♭7
♭7 3 ♭9

D11

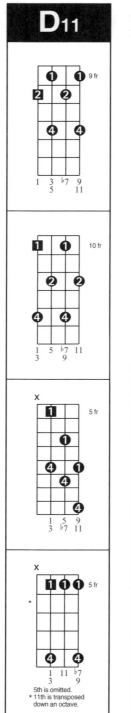

9 fr

1 3 ♭7 9
  5 11

x 10 fr

1 5 ♭7 11
3 9

x 5 fr

1 5 9
3 ♭7 11

x 5 fr

*

1 11 ♭7
3 9

5th is omitted.
* 11th is transposed
down an octave.

D13

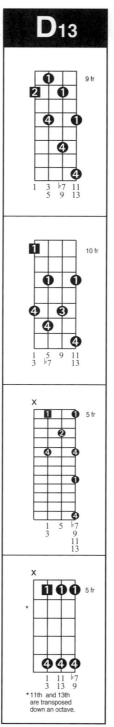

9 fr

1 3 ♭7 11
  5 9 13

10 fr

1 5 9 11
3 ♭7 13

x 5 fr

1 5 ♭7
3 9 11 13

x 5 fr

*

1 11 ♭7
3 13 9

* 11th and 13th
are transposed
down an octave.

D°7

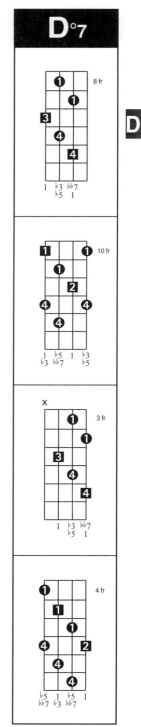

8 fr

1 ♭3 ♭♭7
♭5 1

10 fr

1 ♭5 1 ♭3
♭3 ♭♭7 ♭5

x 3 fr

1 ♭3 ♭♭7
♭5 1

4 fr

♭5 1 ♭5 1
♭♭7 ♭3 ♭♭7

D

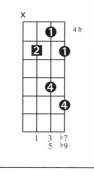

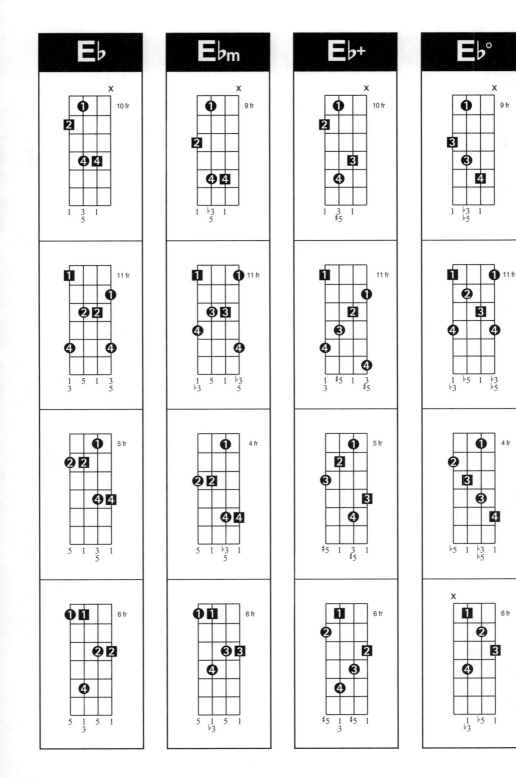

E♭5

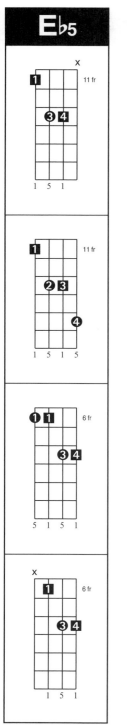

E♭add9

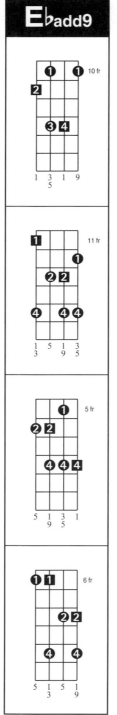

E♭m(add9)

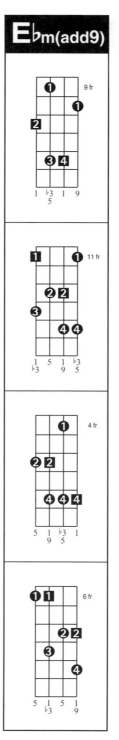

E♭sus4

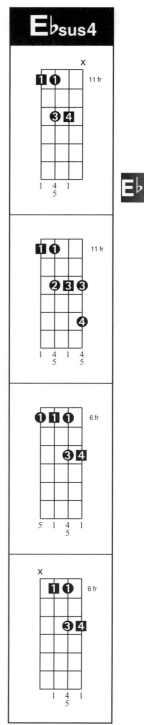

E♭

31

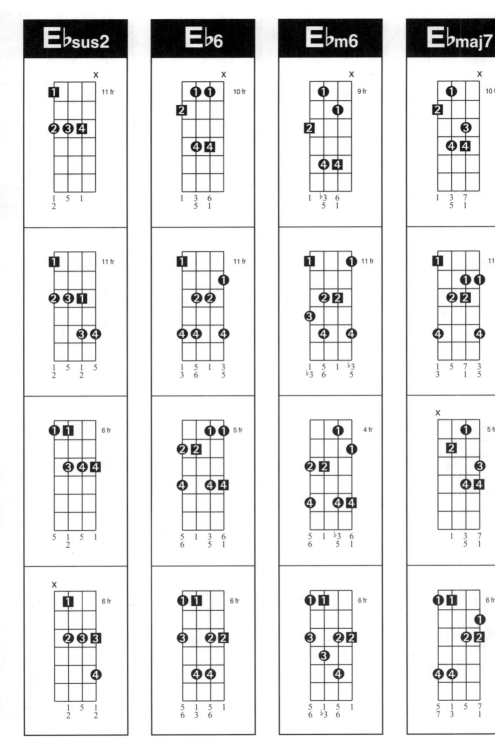

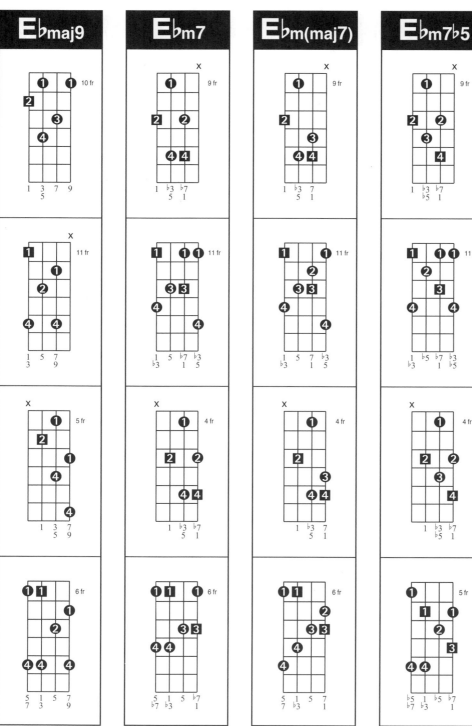

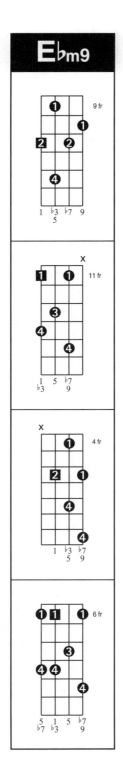
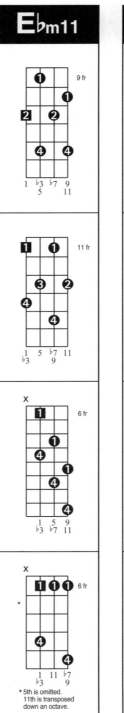
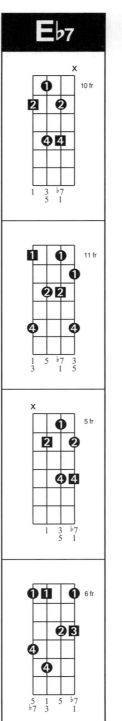
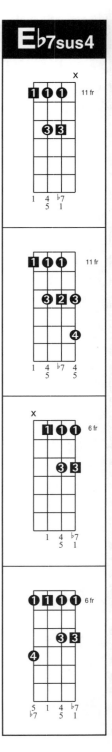

Eb+7 | Eb7b5 | Eb9 | Eb7#9

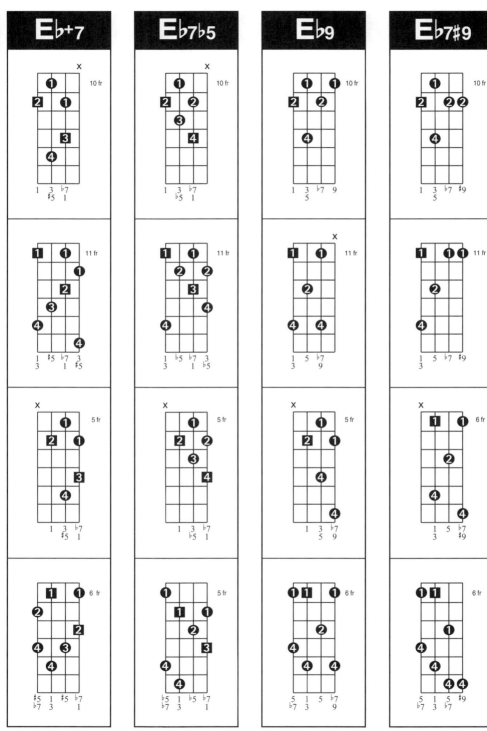

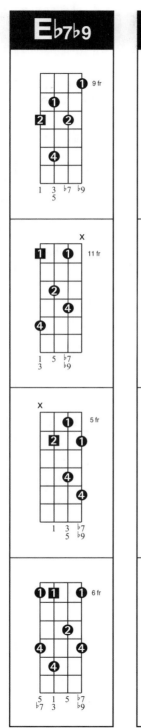

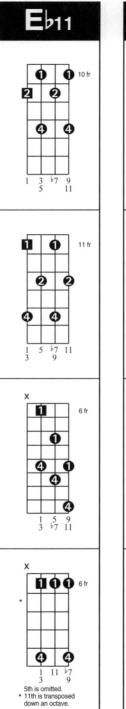

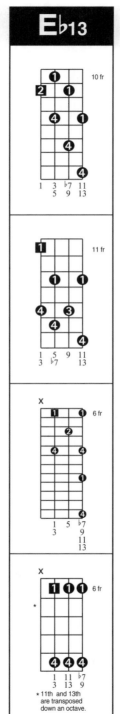

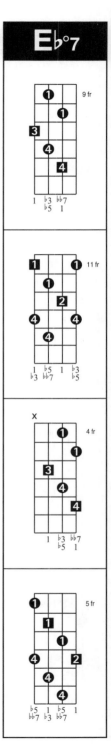

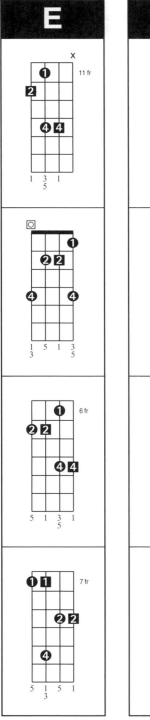
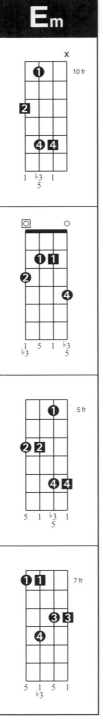
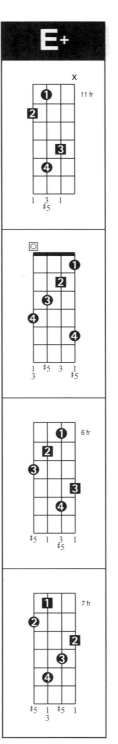
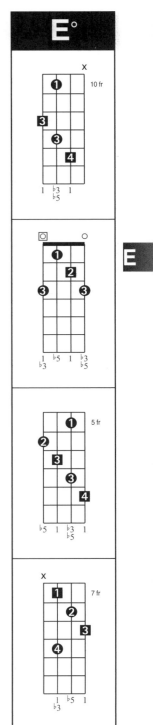

37

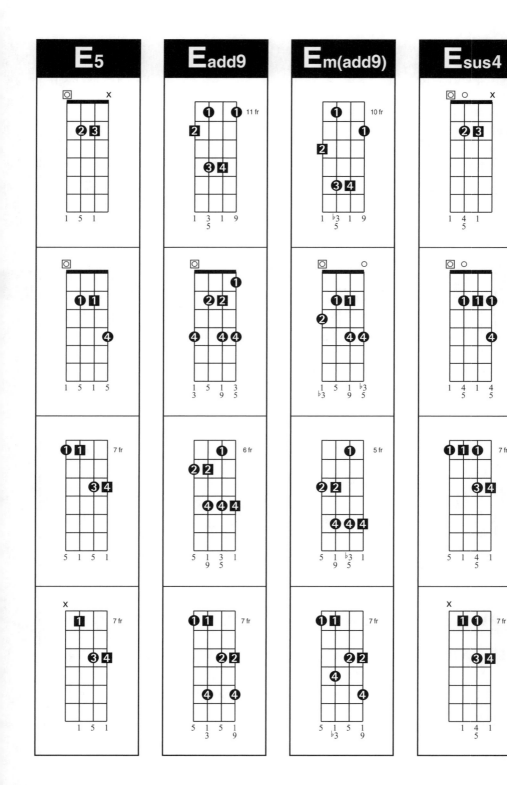

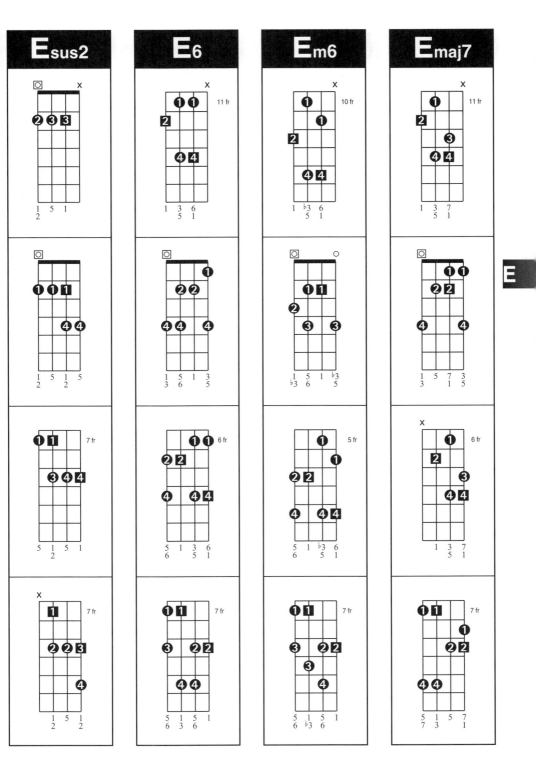

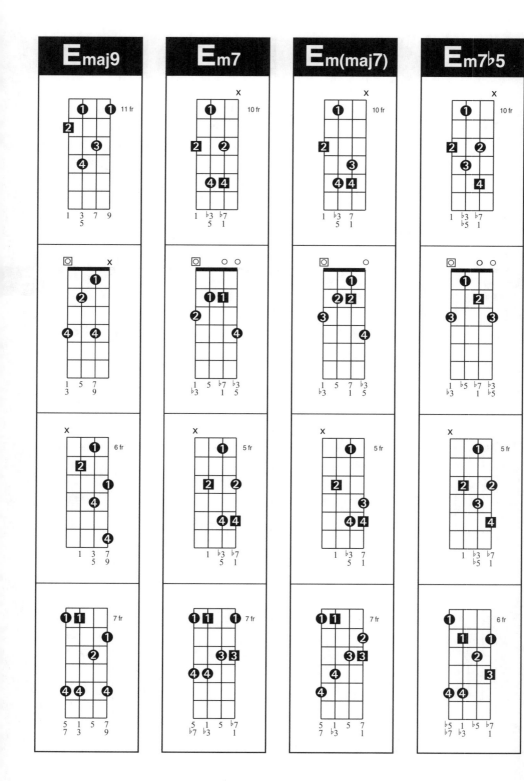

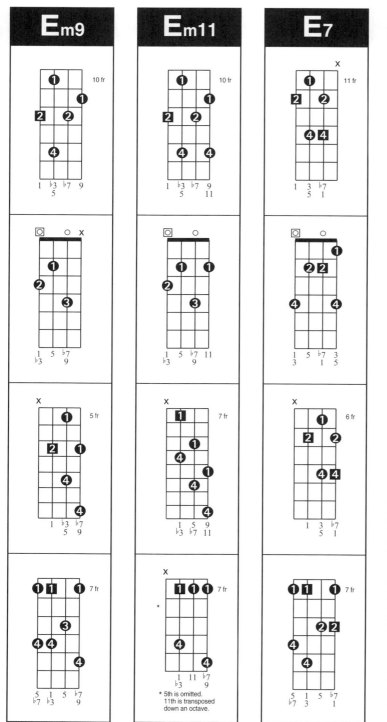

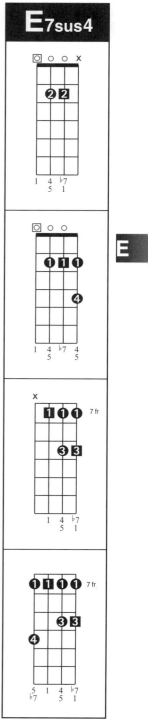

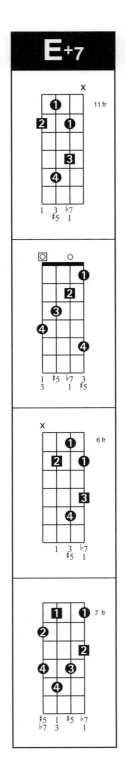
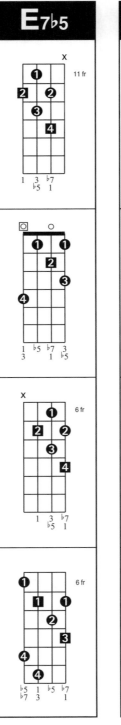
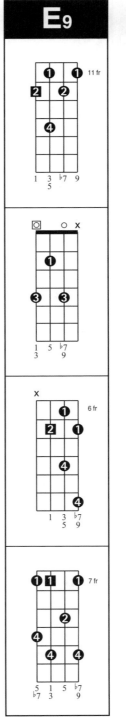
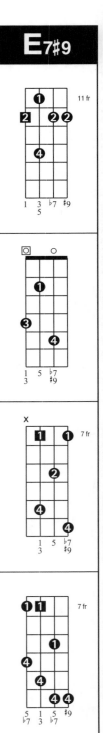

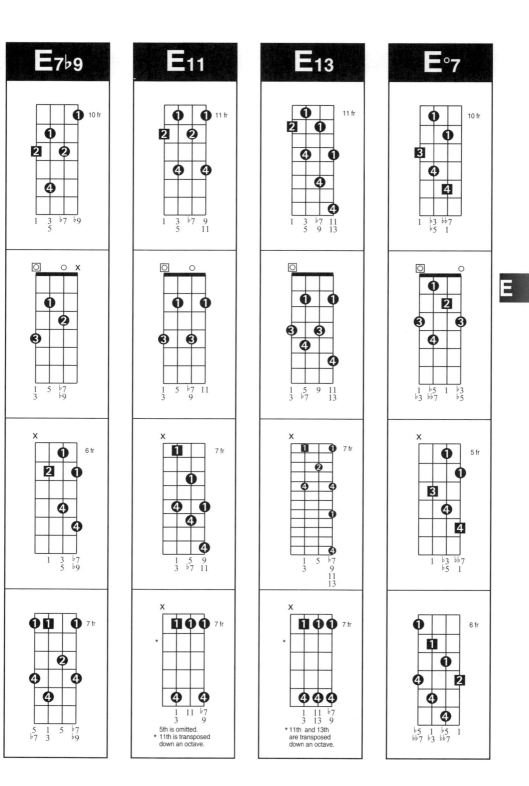

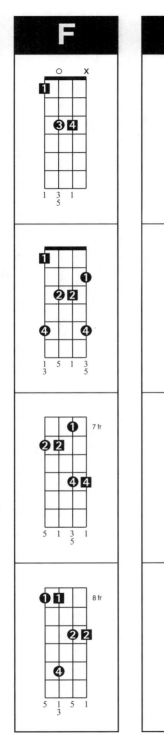
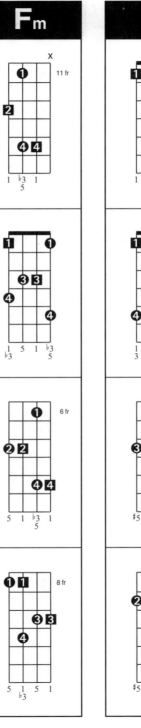
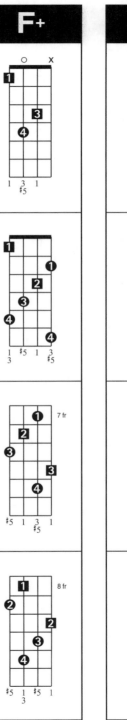
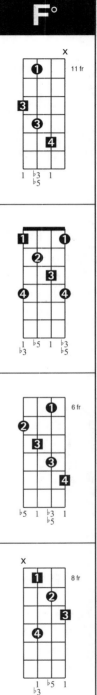

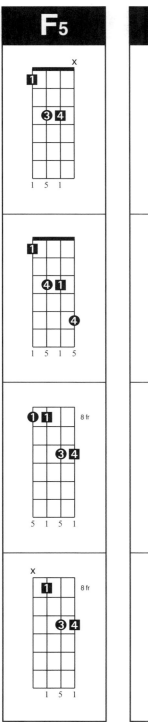
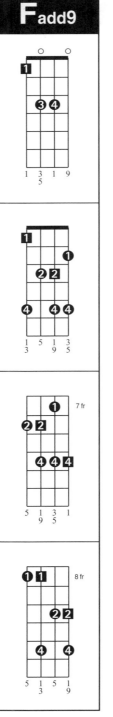
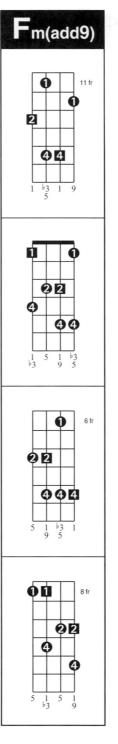
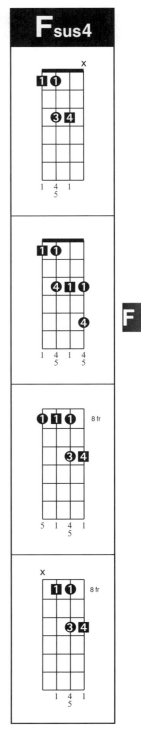

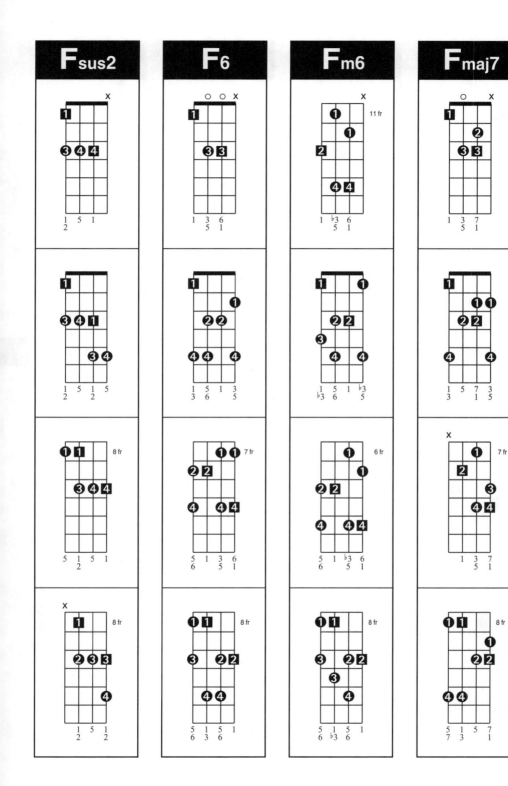

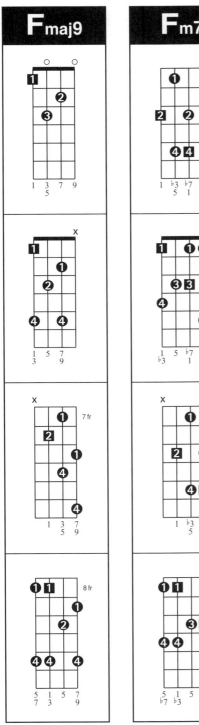
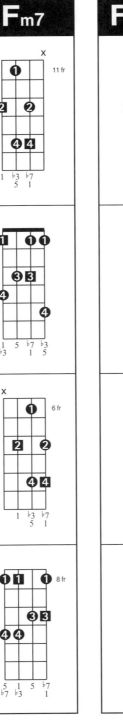
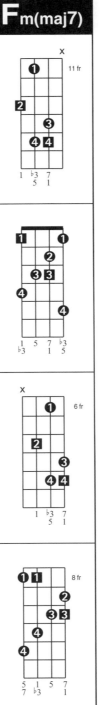
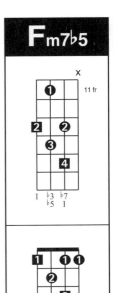
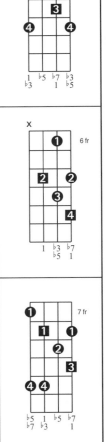

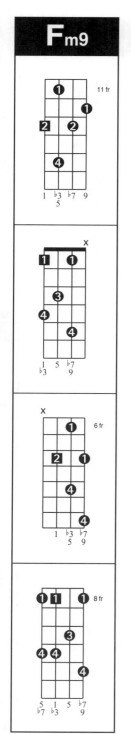

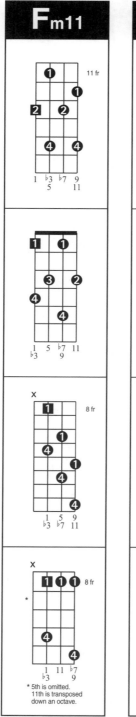

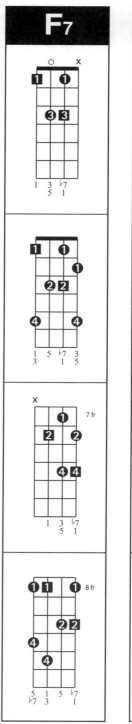

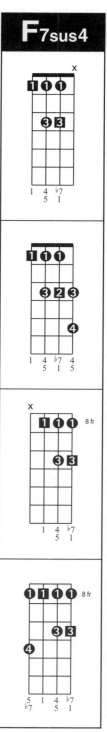

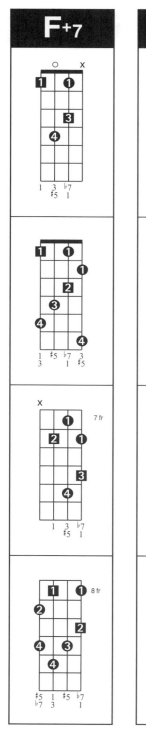

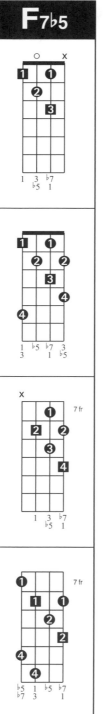

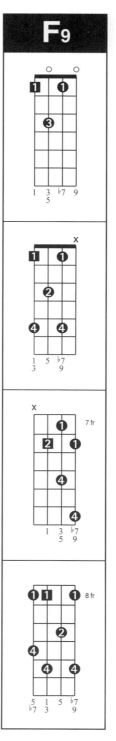

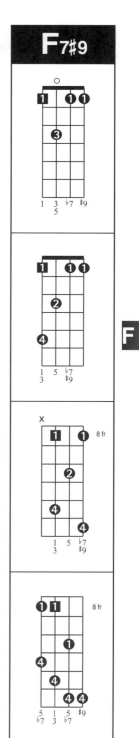

F

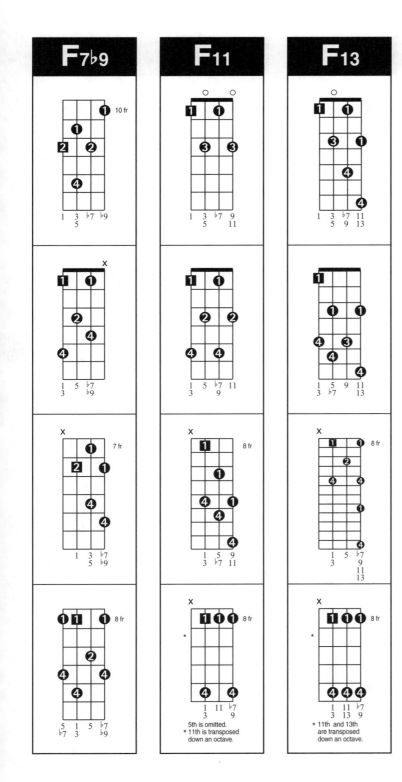
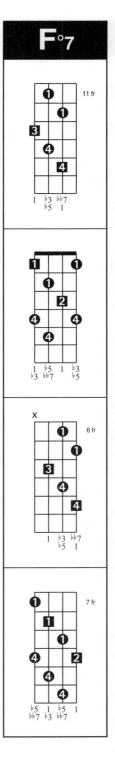

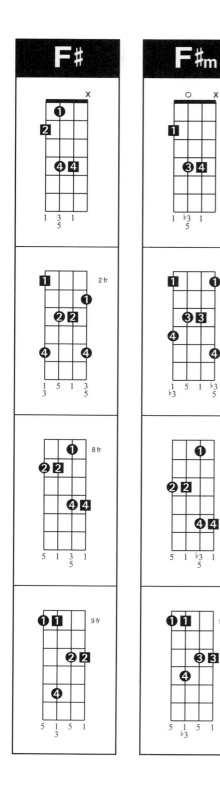

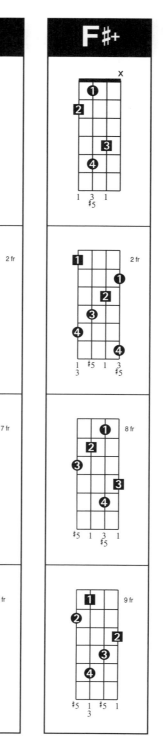

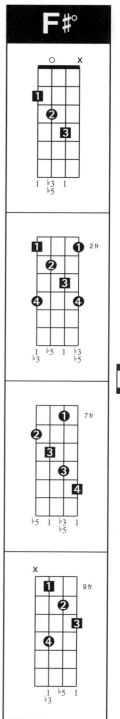

F#

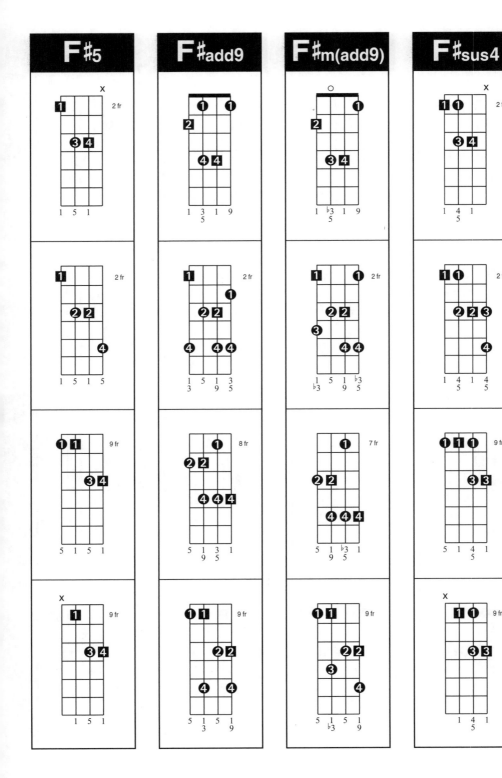

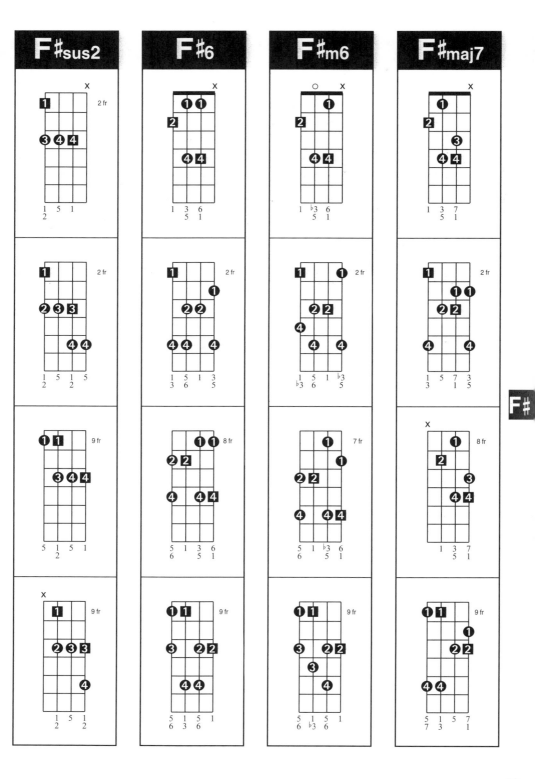

F#sus2 F#6 F#m6 F#maj7

F#

53

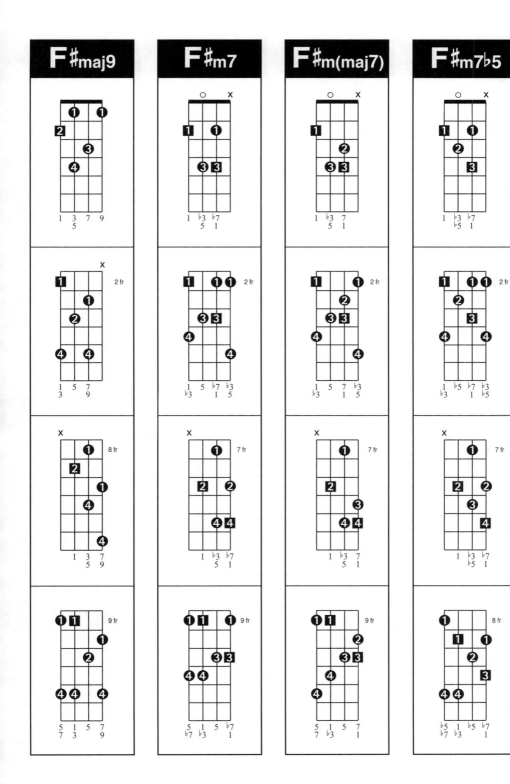

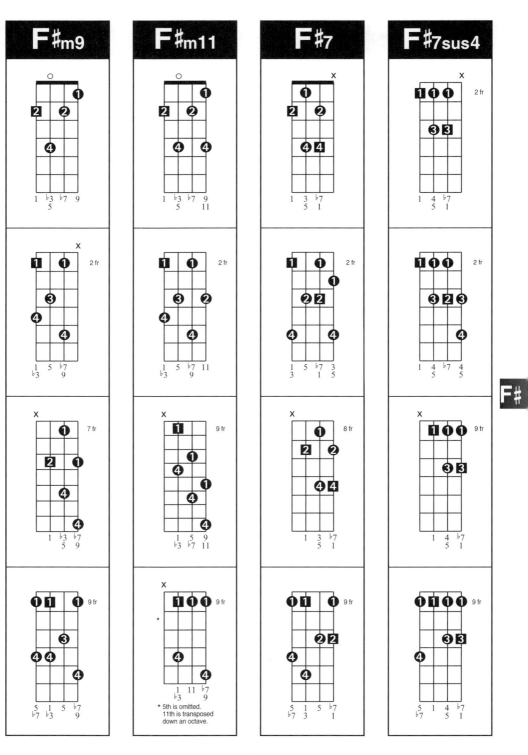

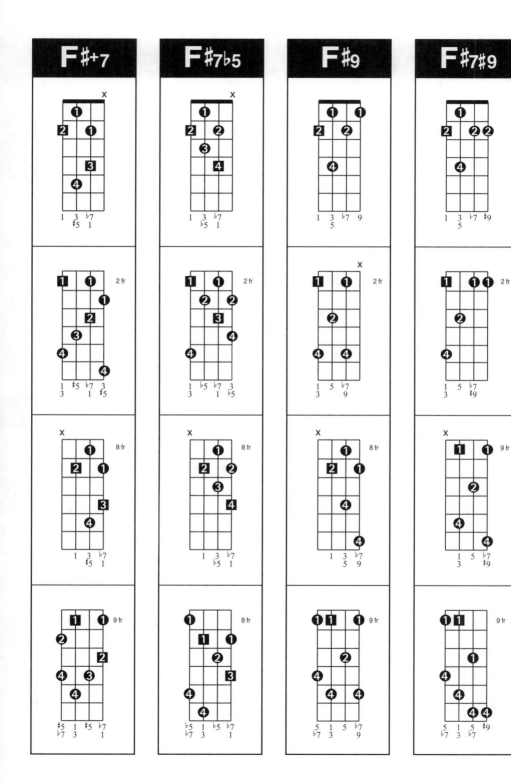

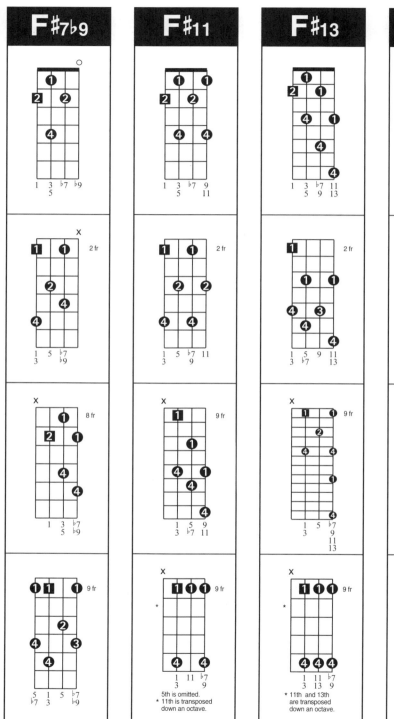
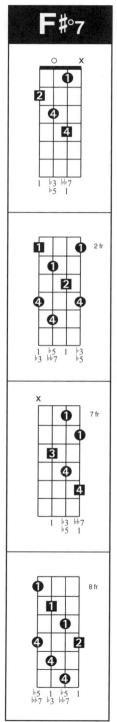

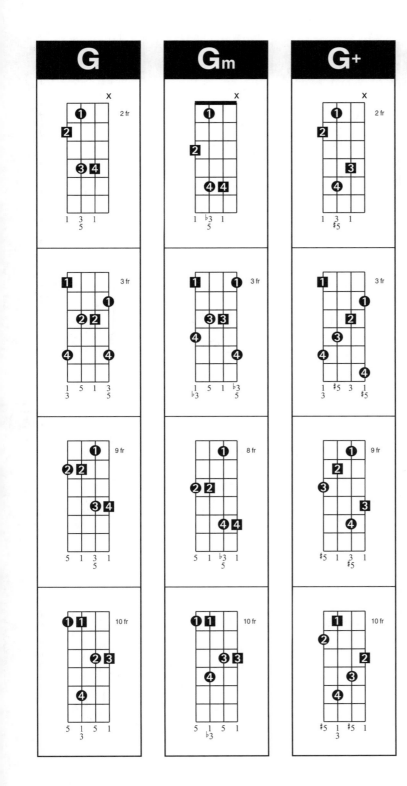
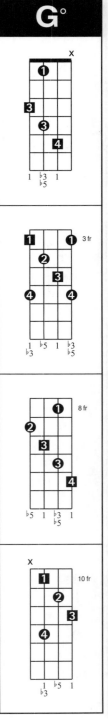

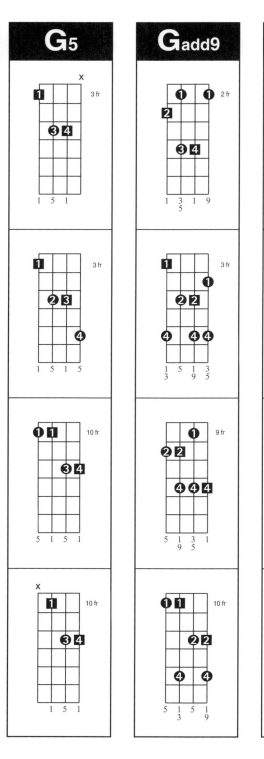

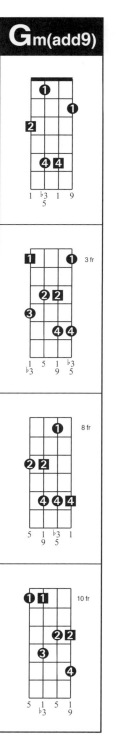

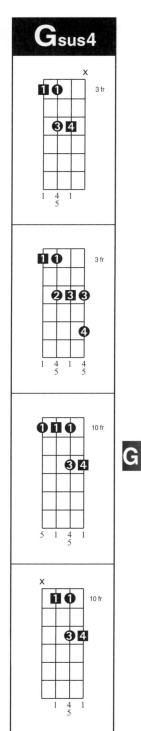

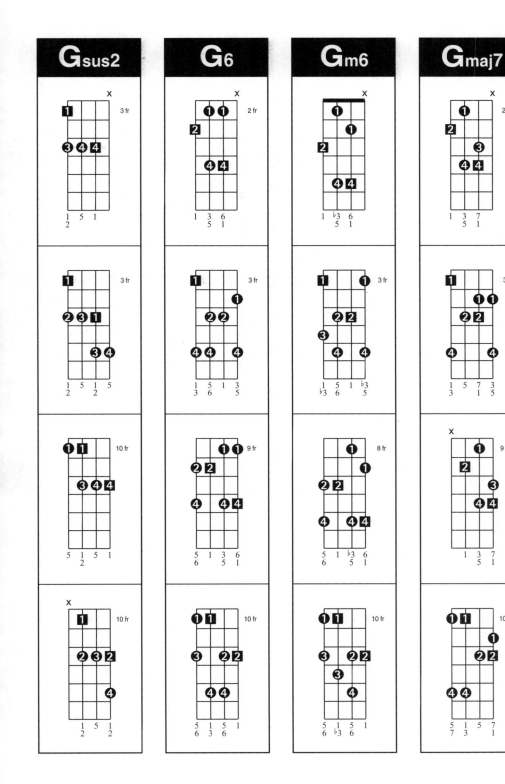

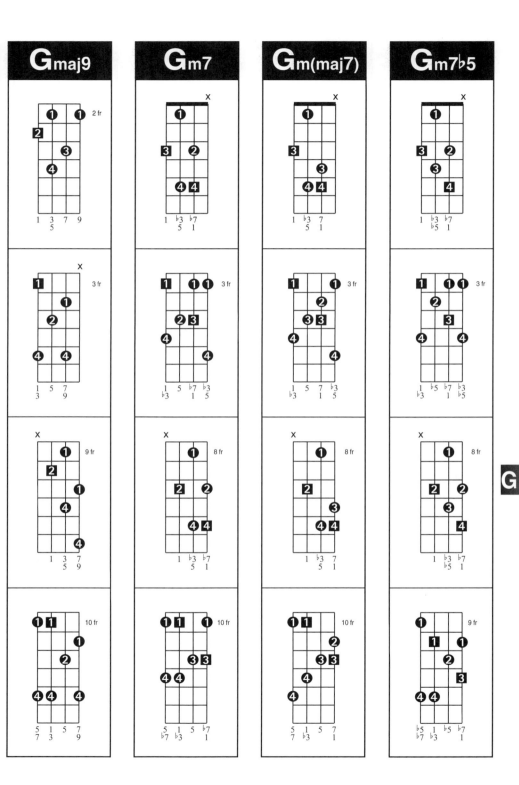

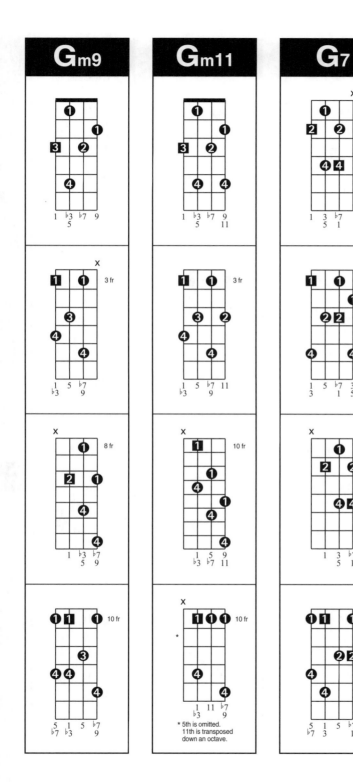
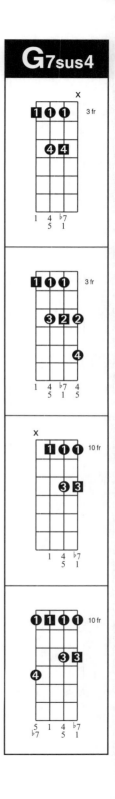

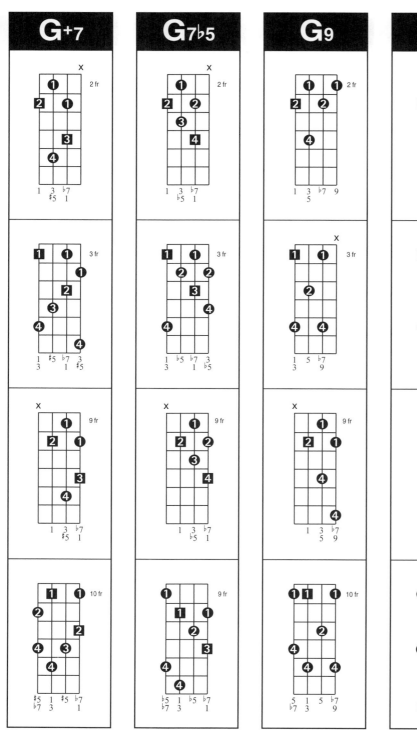
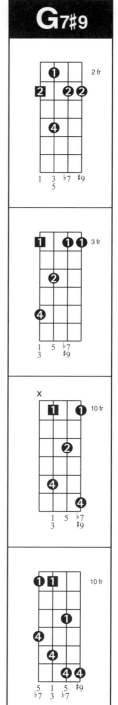

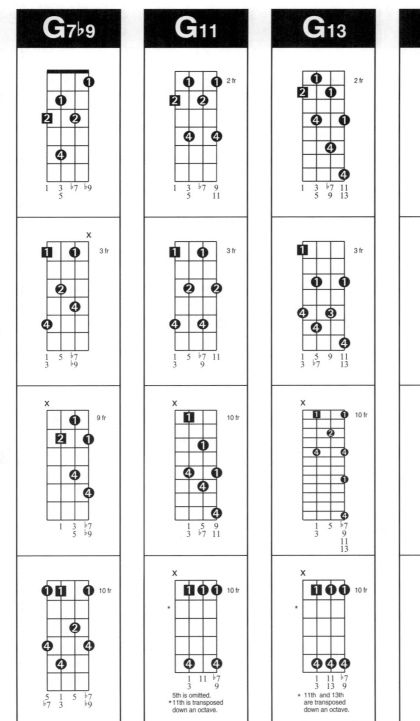
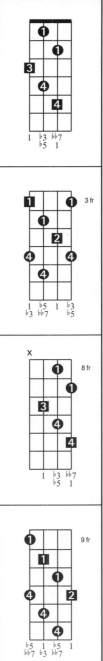

Ab   Abm   Ab+   Ab°

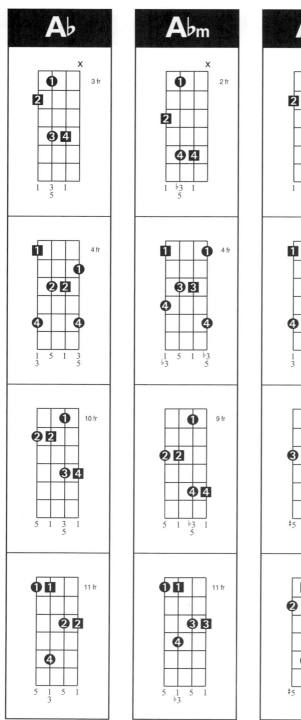
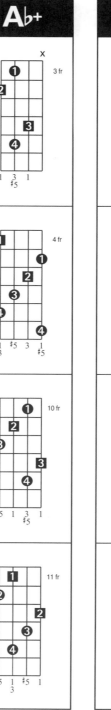
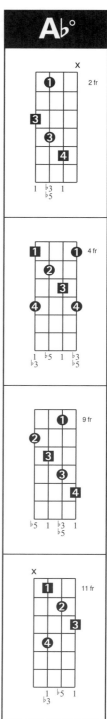

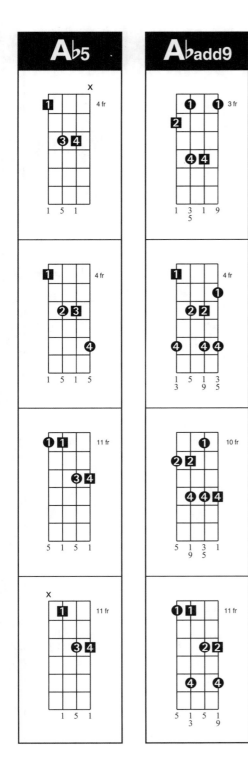
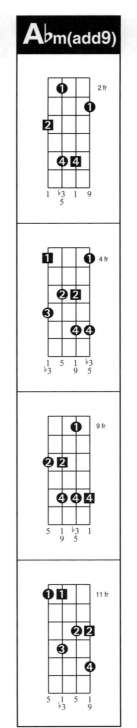
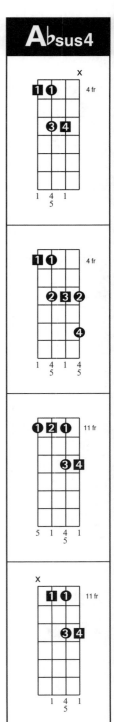

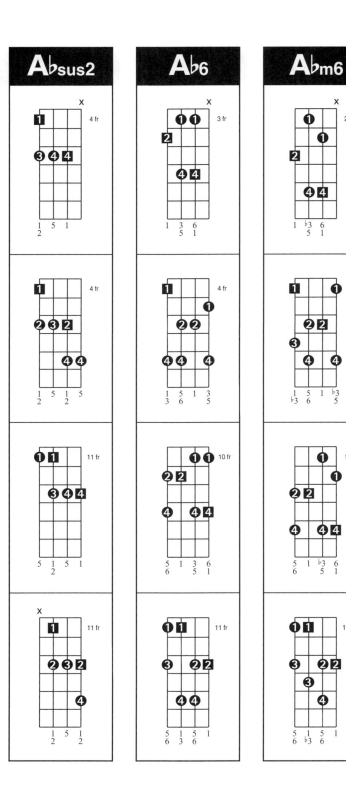

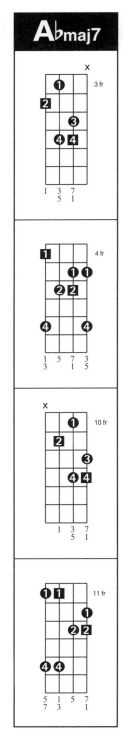

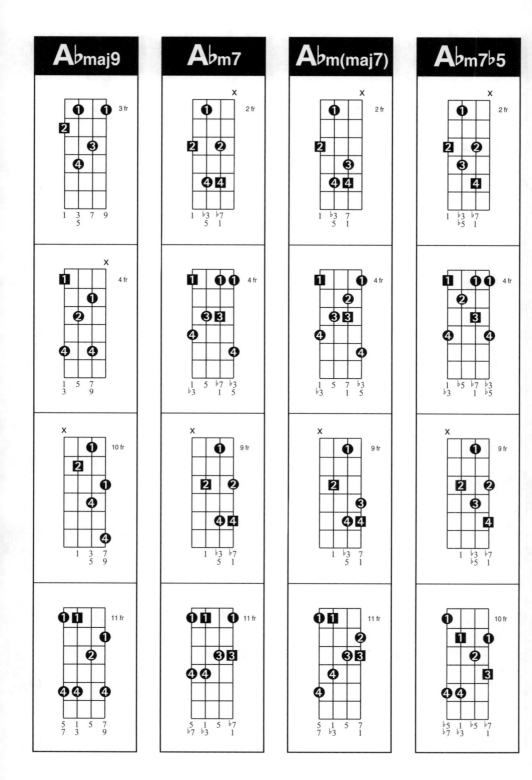

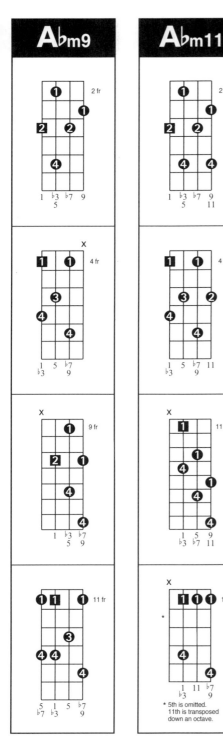
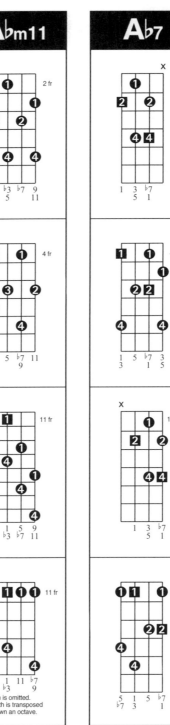
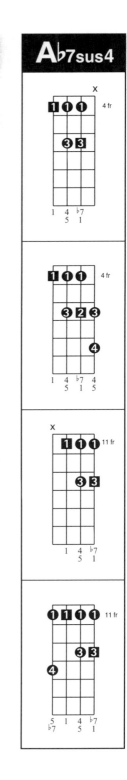

A♭

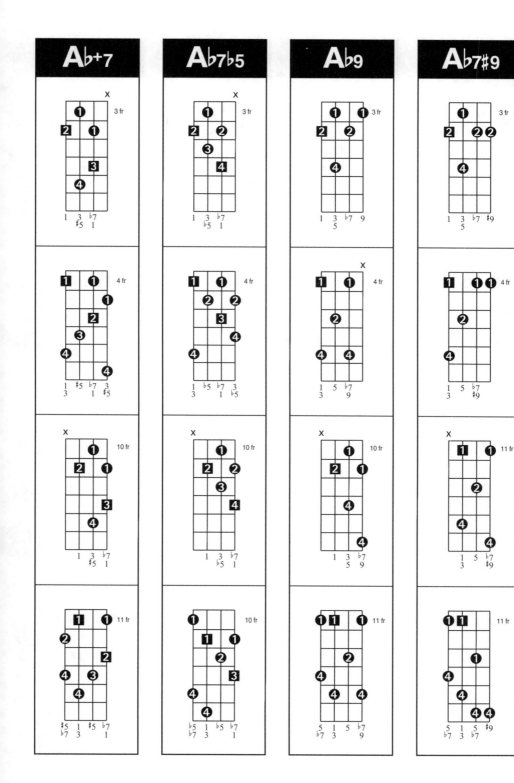

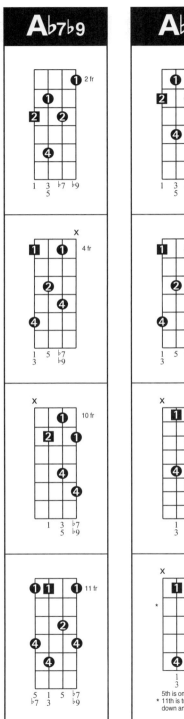

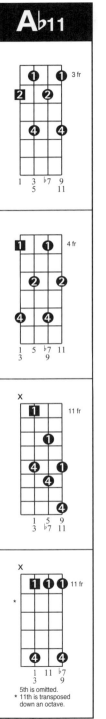

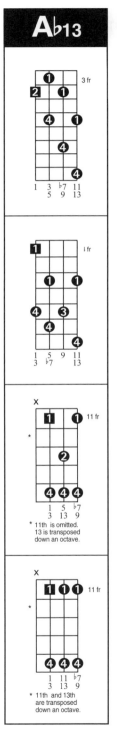

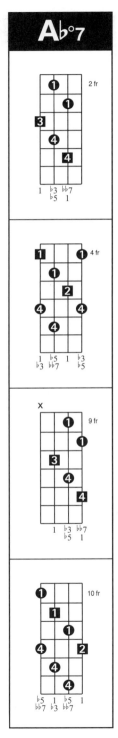

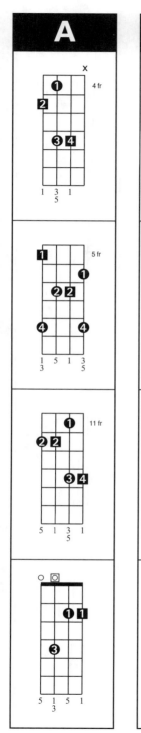
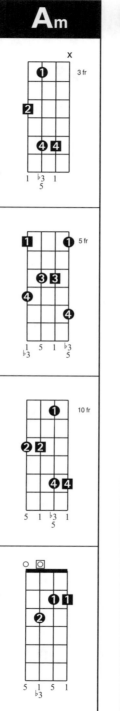
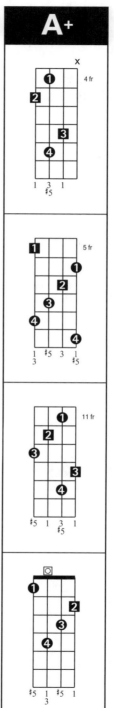
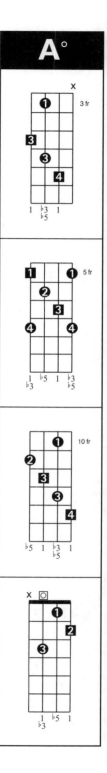

A5　Aadd9　Am(add9)　Asus4

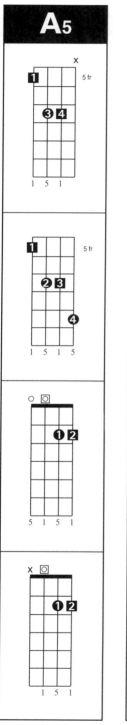
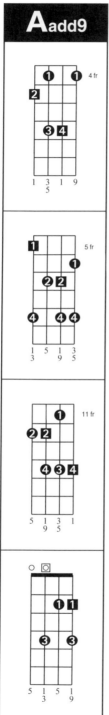
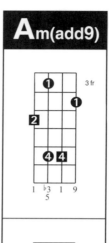
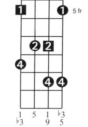
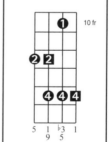
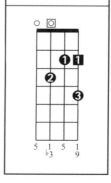
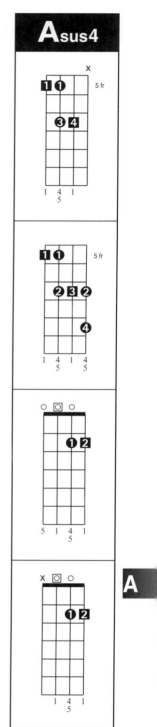

A

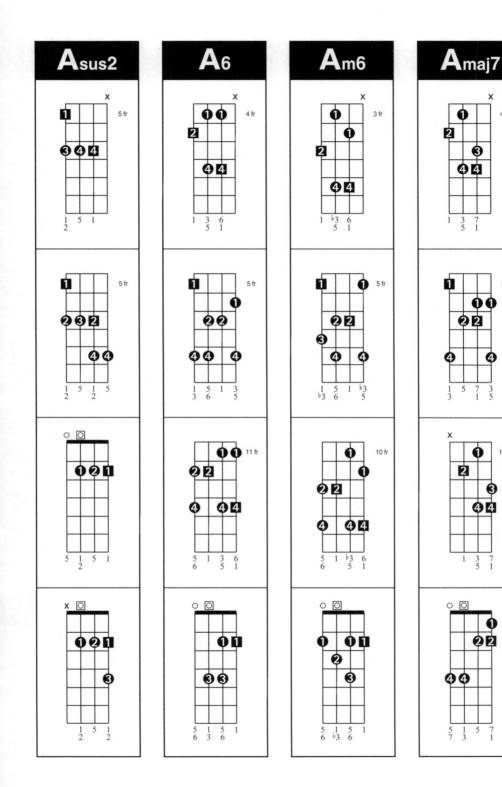

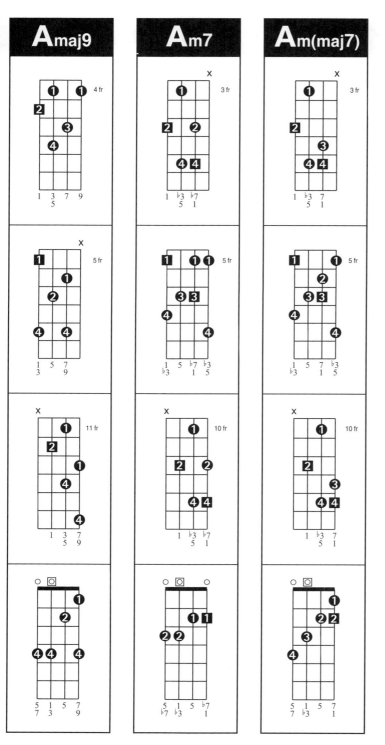
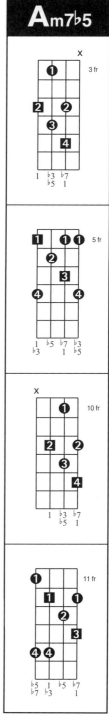

Am9

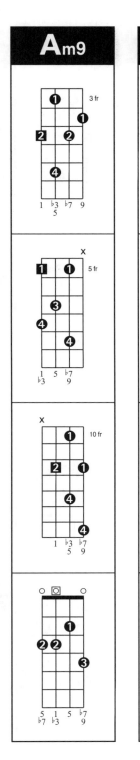

Am11

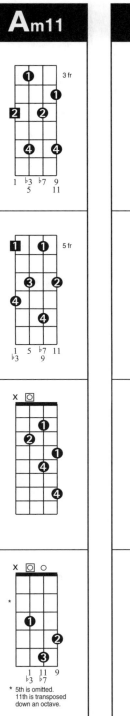

* 5th is omitted.
  11th is transposed
  down an octave.

A7

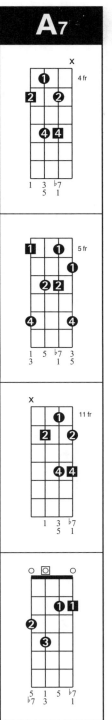

A7sus4

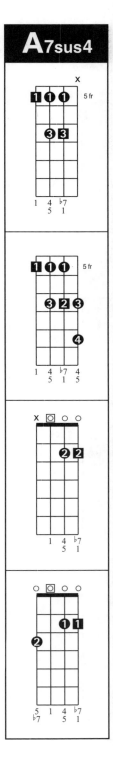

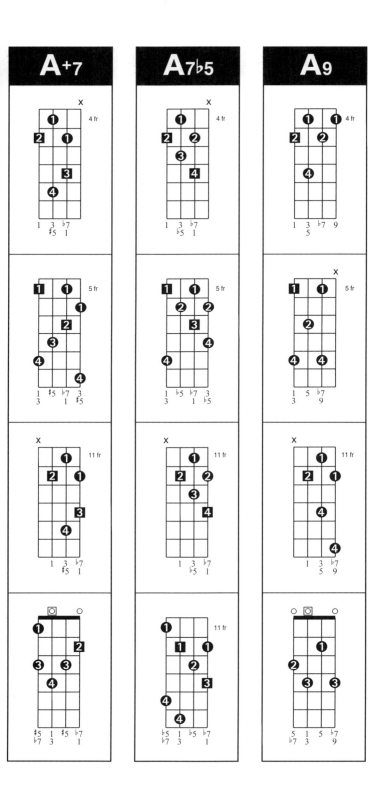
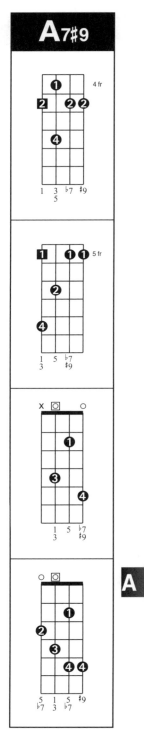

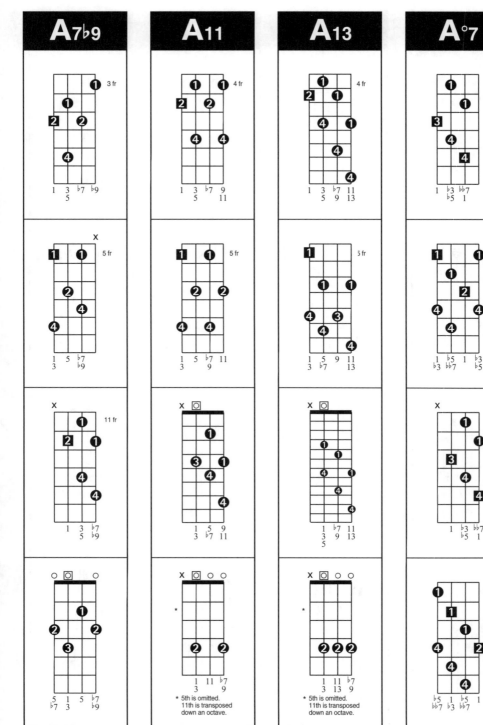

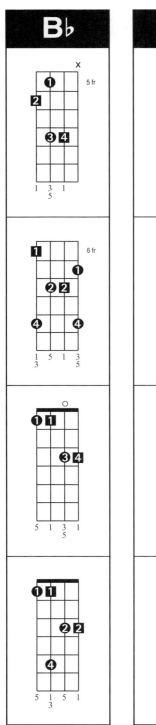
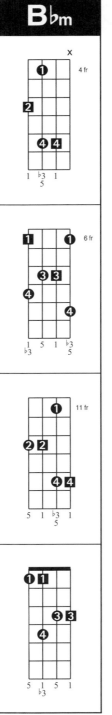
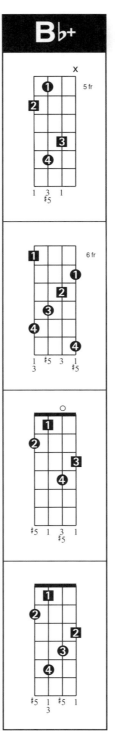
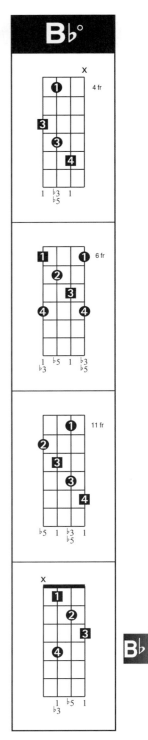

B♭

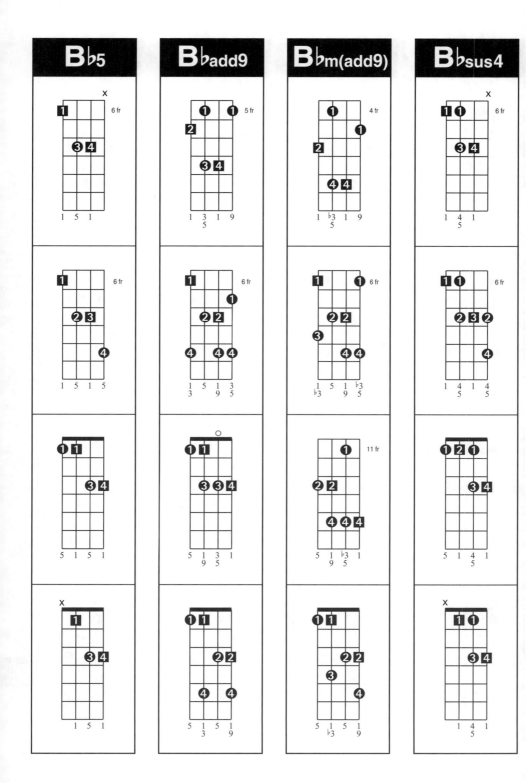

Bb5　Bbadd9　Bbm(add9)　Bbsus4

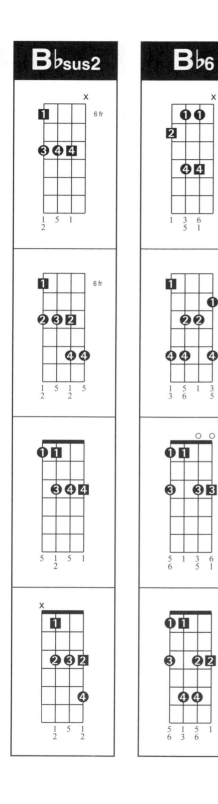

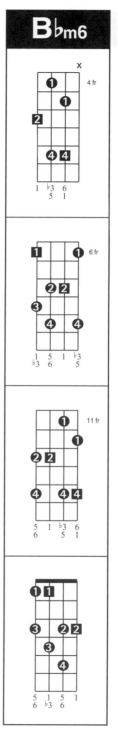

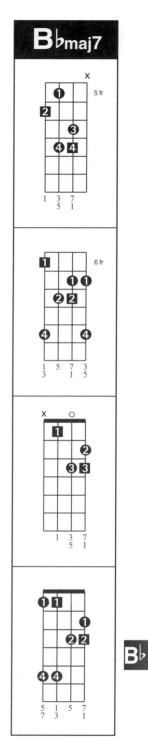

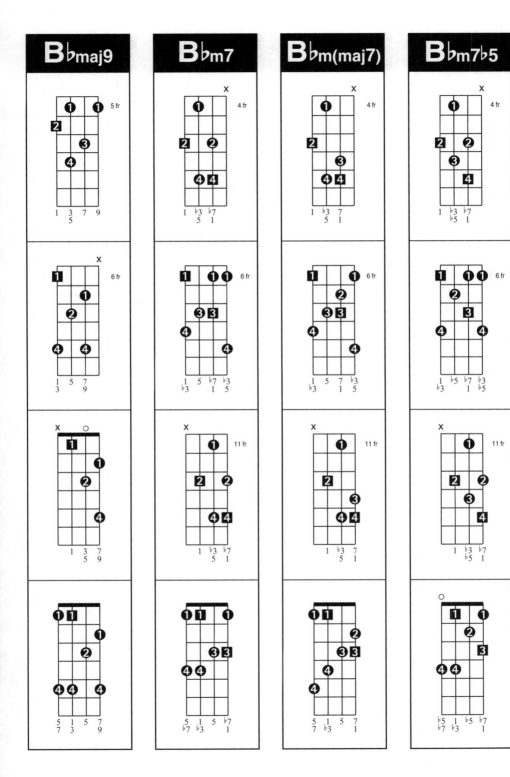

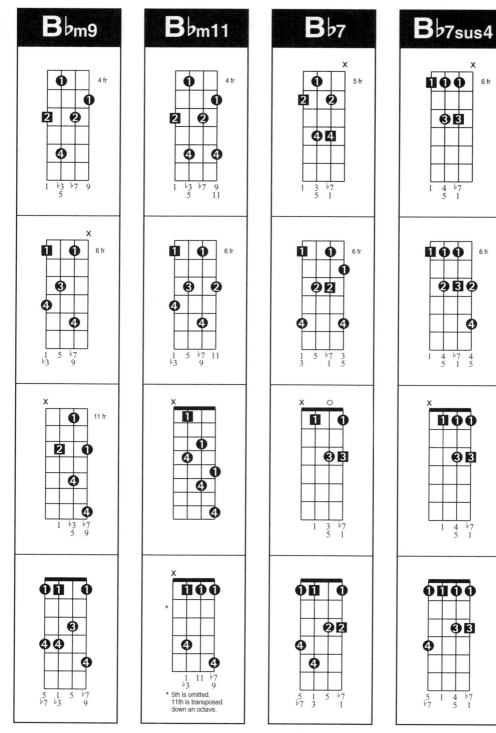

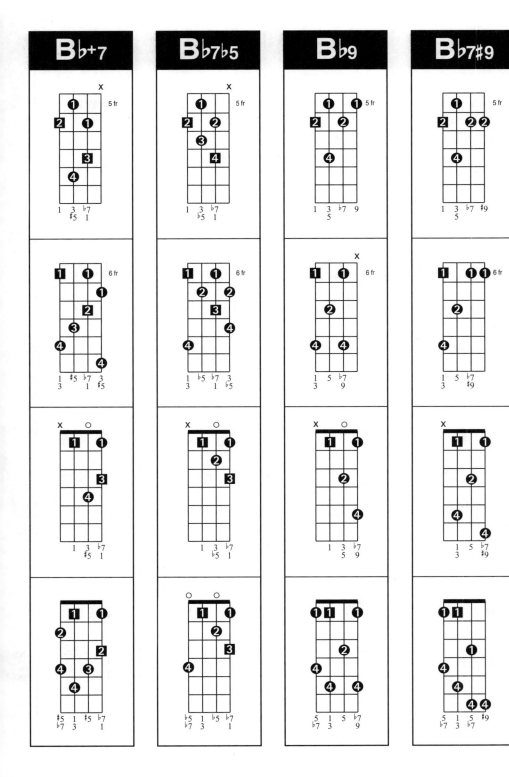

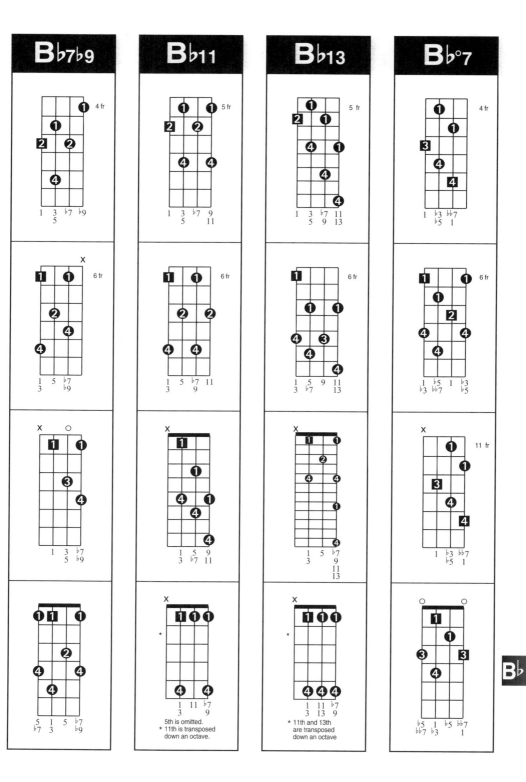

85

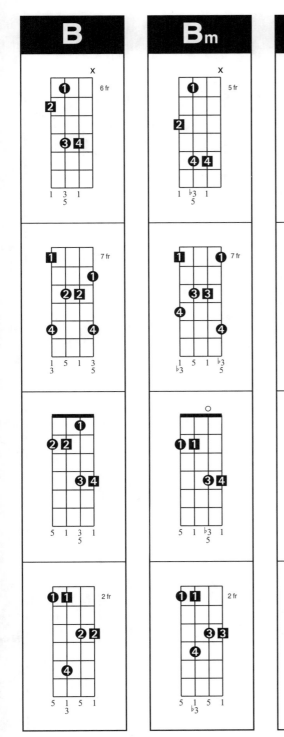
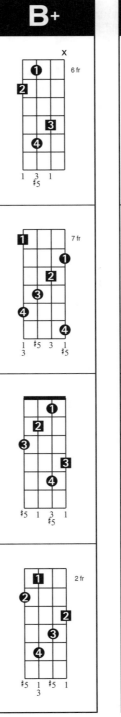
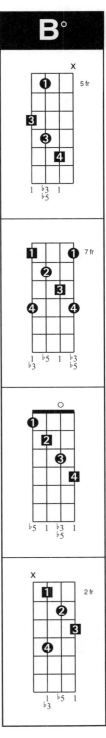

86

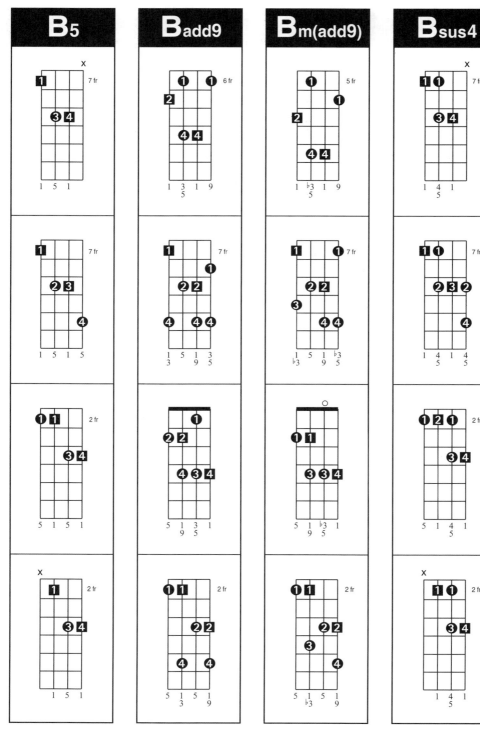

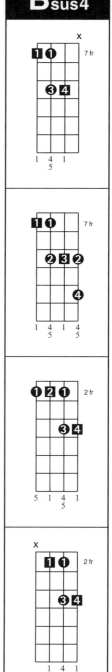

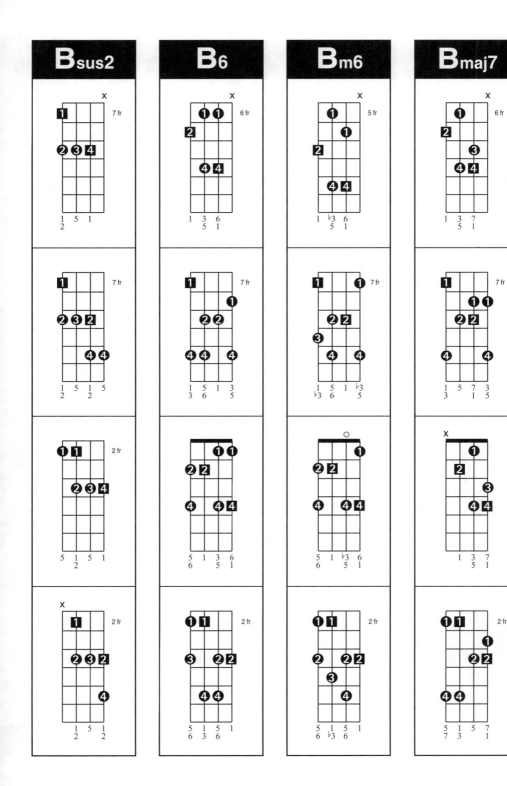

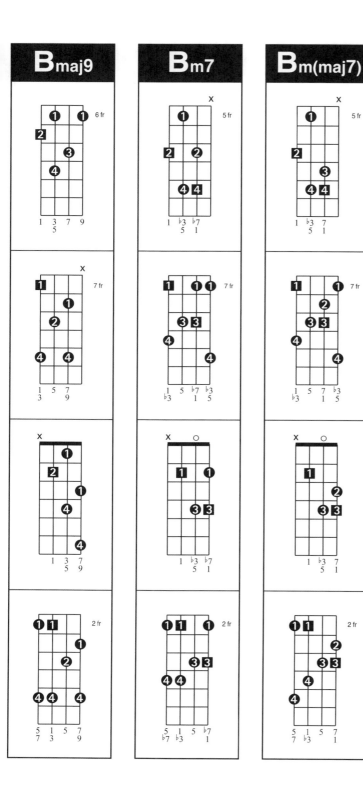
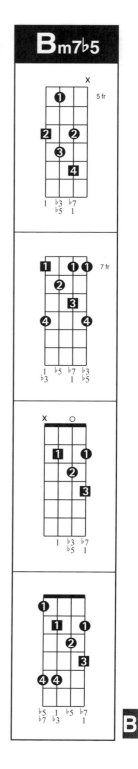

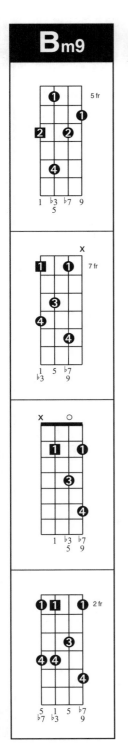

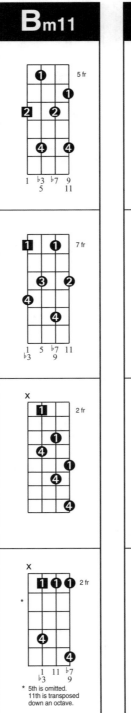

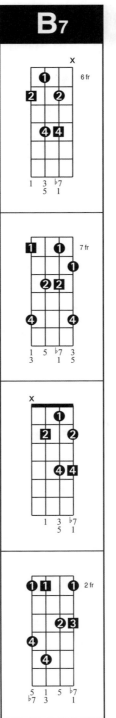

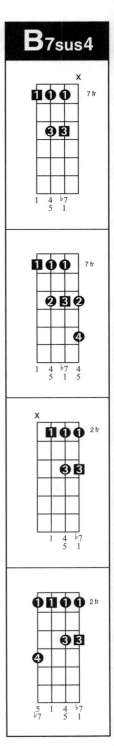

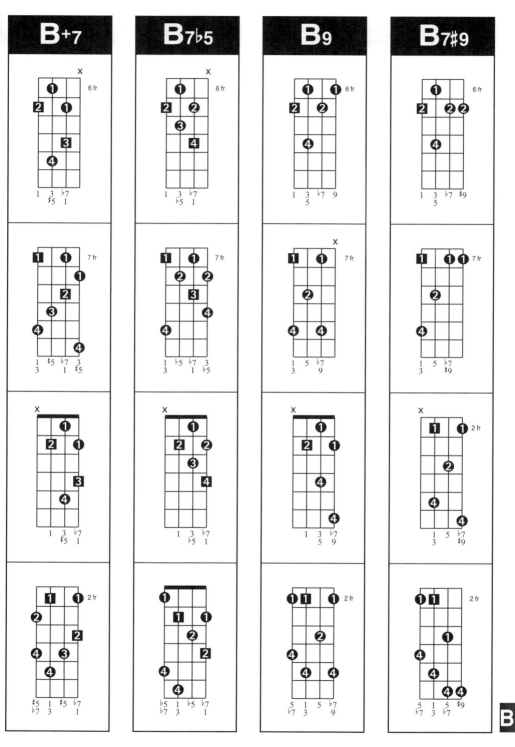

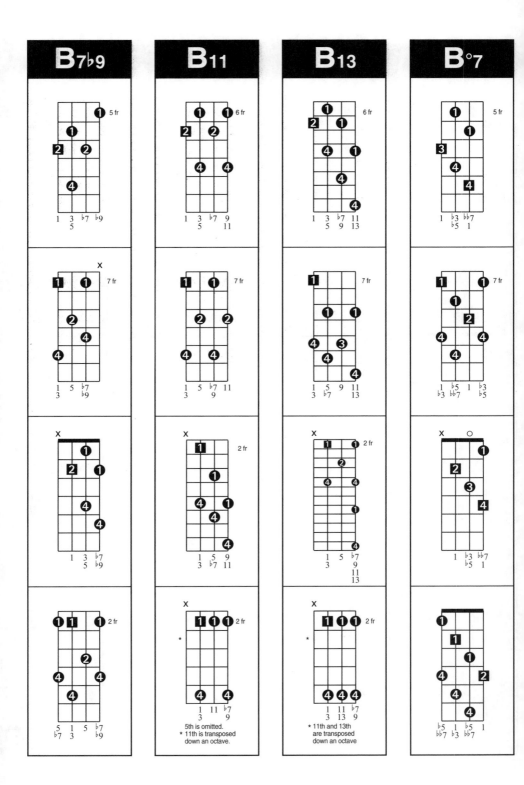

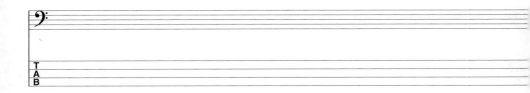